Dear Monsignor Liddy,

Thank you for your support!

Sincerely,
Jack [signature]

America's 'Great Immigrants'
An Analysis of Carnegie Corporation's Honorees, 2006-2015

Adonis & Abbey Publishers Ltd
St James House
13 Kensington Square,
London, W8 5HD
United Kingdom

Website: http://www.adonis-abbey.com
E-mail Address: editor@adonis-abbey.com

Nigeria:
Suites C4 & C5 J-Plus Plaza
Asokoro, Abuja, Nigeria
Tel: +234 (0) 7058078841/08052035034

Copyright 2017 © Amadu Jacky Kaba

British Library Cataloguing-in-Publication Data
A catalogue record for this book is available from the British Library

ISBN: 978-1-909112-78-0

The moral right of the author has been asserted

All rights reserved. No part of this book may be reproduced, stored in a retrieval system or transmitted at any time or by any means without the prior permission of the publisher

America's 'Great Immigrants'
An Analysis of Carnegie Corporation's Honorees, 2006-2015

Amadu Jacky Kaba

TABLE OF CONTENTS

Dedication... viii

CHAPTER ONE
Introduction 9

CHAPTER TWO:
(Re)Conceptualizing the Brain Drain Phenomenon as Competition....... 13

CHAPTER THREE
Methodology, Data Availability, Reliability, and Limitations of this
Study 19

CHAPTER FOUR:
Findings/Results and Analysis 22
    Gender/Sex 22

Table 1. Carnegie Corporation of New York's "Pride of America"
Honorees, by Sex: 2006-2015 22

Racial Background of "Pride of America" Honorees,
2006-2015 23
Table 2. Carnegie Corporation of New York's "Pride of America"

Honorees, by Race and Sex: 2006-2015 24

Month of Birth of Carnegie Corporation of New York's "Pride of
America" Honorees, by Race and Sex, 2006-2015 25

Table 3. Month of Birth of Carnegie Corporation of New York's
"Pride of America" Honorees, by Race and Sex, 2006-2015 26

Year of Birth of Carnegie Corporation of New York's "Pride of
America" Honorees, by Race and Sex, 2006-2015 27

Table 4. Year of Birth of Carnegie Corporation of New York's
"Pride of America" Honorees, by Race and Sex, 2006-2015 28

Previous Nationality/Citizenship of Carnegie Corporation of New
York's "Pride of America" Honorees, by Race and Sex,
2006-2015 31

Table 5. Previous Nationality/Citizenship of Carnegie
Corporation of New York's "Pride of America" Honorees,
by Race and Sex, 2006-2015 33

Geographic Region of Previous Country of Citizenship of
Carnegie Corporation of New York's "Pride of America"
Honorees, by Race and Sex, 2006-2015 37

Table 6. Geographic Region of Previous Country of Citizenship of
Carnegie Corporation of New York's "Pride of America"
Honorees, by Race and Sex, 2006-2015 38

List of Previous Nationality/Country, their U.S. Population,
Country's Population, GDP, and GDP Per Capita of Carnegie
Corporation of New York's "Pride of America"
Honorees, 2006-2015 40

Table 7. List of Previous Nationality/Country, their U.S. Ancestry
Population, Country's Population, GDP, and GDP Per Capita of
Carnegie Corporation of New York's "Pride of America"
Honorees, 2006-2015 42

Educational Attainment (Highest/Terminal Higher Education
Degree Earned) of "Pride of America" Honorees, 2006-2015 47

Table 8. Levels and Types of Earned Highest/Terminal Higher
Education Degrees by Carnegie Corporation of New York's "Pride
of America" Honorees, by Race and Sex, 2006-2015 49

Academic Major of Earned Highest/Terminal Higher Education
Degrees Earned by Carnegie Corporation of New York's "Pride of
America" Honorees, by Race and Sex, 2006-2015 51

Table 9. Academic Major of Earned Highest/Terminal Higher Education Degrees of Carnegie Corporation of New York's "Pride of America" Honorees, by Race and Sex, 2006-2015 54

Year of Graduation from Higher Education Institutions by Carnegie Corporation of New York's "Pride of America" Honorees, by Race and Sex, 2006-2015 60

Table 10 Year of Graduation from Higher Education Institutions by Carnegie Corporation of New York's "Pride of America" Honorees, by Race and Sex, 2006-2015 62

Academic Institutions where Highest/Terminal Higher Education Degrees are earned by Carnegie Corporation of New York's "Pride of America" Honorees, by Race and Sex, 2006-2015 71

Table 11. Academic Institutions Where Highest/Terminal Higher Education Degrees Were Earned by Carnegie Corporation of New York's "Pride of America" Honorees, by Race and Sex, 2006-2015 74

U.S. State/Country and Geographic Region of Earned Highest/Terminal Higher Education Degrees by Carnegie Corporation of New York's "Pride of America" Honorees, by Race and Sex, 2006-2015 84

Table 12. U.S. State/Country of Earned Highest/Terminal Higher Education Degrees of Carnegie Corporation of New York's "Pride of America" Honorees, by Race and Sex, 2006-2015 90

Table 13. World Region where Academic Degrees were earned by Carnegie Corporation of New York's "Pride of America" Honorees, by Sex, 2006-2015 99

Net Worth of a Selected Number of "Pride of America" Honorees (n=122) 101

Table 14. Net Worth of Carnegie Corporation of New York's "Pride of America" Honorees, by Sex, 2006-2015 (as of mid-November 2015 and before) 102

CHAPTER FIVE
Discussion 105

CHAPTER SIX
Conclusion 113

REFERENCES 115

APPENDIXES 125

Table A1. Name, Previous Country/Nationality, and Profession of Carnegie Corporation's "Pride of America" Honorees, 2006-2015 125

Table A2. "Pride of America" Honorees who are Nobel Laureates, Field, Year, Race and Previous Nationality, 2006-2015 142

Table A3. Net Worth of Carnegie Corporation of New York's "Pride of America" Honorees, by Sex, 2006-2015 144

INDEX 149

DEDICATED TO

Andzi, Fudia Christina and Siri Mahan

CHAPTER ONE

INTRODUCTION

Immigrants in the United States, regardless of gender, race, or educational background, tend to go through the normal challenges of being immigrants (Shenoy-Packer, 2015; Timberlake & Williams, 2012). However, the years 2015 and 2016 will be remembered in decades to come for the very strong anti-immigrant language among leading Republican presidential contenders for the 2016 presidential election. Whether based on religion, ethnicity, race, or education level, immigrants suffered serious negative criticisms from these leading candidates ("A Prison is a Prison," 2015: 528; Boot, 2016; Chavez, 2015; Chopra, 2016; Figueroa-Santana, 2015: 2222; Goutor, 2015; Jaret & Kolozsvari-Wright, 2011: 196; Lal, 2015; Ziabari, 2016ab). However, without immigrants, including those who arrived during the past decade, the United States would not continue to play a leading role in the world in innovation and many other important aspects of civilization. Immigrants are among the country's most important employers, employing millions of people. Among the people who have helped the U.S. remain the leading (or a leading) nation in science, technology, arts, politics, etc. are immigrants from hundreds of nations or countries (Campanella, 2015; Chilea & Kassai, 2015; Hunt, 2011; Kaba, 2011a; Kerr & Lincoln, 2010; Kim et al., 2011; McDowell & Singell, Jr., 2000; No & Walsh, 2010; Teich, 2014; Wadhwa, 2009; Webber, 2012).

The Carnegie Corporation of New York established the "Great Immigrants: The Pride of America" program to honor these individuals' contributions to the greatness of the United States. Andrew Carnegie himself, in whose name this program is established, was an immigrant from Scotland. From 2006 to 2015, the Carnegie Corporation has honored hundreds of naturalized Americans who have made substantial contributions to the United States and the world. Among the over 400 honorees during this period are a number of individuals who have been honored posthumously, including Nobel

Laureate Albert Einstein and Isaac Asimov, an author and professor of biochemistry at Boston University.

Table A1 (see appendixes section) lists the names of all 408 honorees, their previous country of citizenship or nationality, and profession, as presented on the Carnegie Corporation's "Great Immigrants" website. The honorees are from all walks of life: actors/actresses; professional athletes; authors; journalists and editors of major newspapers, magazines and television stations; college professors and administrators, including presidents, provosts, and deans of the leading colleges and universities in the U.S.; ambassadors, civil servants, and politicians; heads of Fortune 500 companies, including one of the founders and CEOs of Google, and business leaders and investors; medical doctors; lawyers and judges; musicians, entertainers and dancers; astronauts; poets; museum directors; leaders of the U.S. military; engineers; architects; chefs; philanthropists; sculptors; activists; fashion designers; and fashion models. Among these 408 honorees are winners of important national and international awards. For example, I identified 24 Nobel Laureates.

Table A2 (see appendixes section) presents the names, races, previous nationalities or citizenships, and years the Nobel Prizes were won by the 24 Nobel Laureates. According to Table A2, 9 (37.5%) honorees won in physics: Willard Boyle, 2009; Albert Einstein, 1921; Riccardo Giacconi, 2002; Ivar Giaever, 1973; Charles K. Kao, 2009; Tsung-Dao Lee, 1957; Yoichiro Nambu, 2008; Daniel Tsui, 1998; and Chen-Ning Yang, 1957. Eight (33.3%) of them won in physiology or medicine: Elizabeth H. Blackburn, 2009; Günter Blobel, 1999; Roger Guillemin, 1977; Eric Kandel, 2000; Har Gobind Khorana, 1968; Oliver Smithies, 2007; Thomas C. Südhof, 2013; and Jack Szostak, 2009. Four (16.7%) of them won in chemistry: Walter Kohn, 1998; Mario Molina, 1995; Arieh Warshel, 2013; and Ahmed Zewail, 1999. Finally, 3 (12.5%) of them won in peace: Henry Kissinger, 1973; Bernard Lown, 1985; and Elie Wiesel, 1986 (Table A2; also see Bruner, 2011). Shachar and Hirschl (2013) note that of the over 300 Nobel Prizes awarded from 1901 to 2010 to researchers in the United States, immigrants won almost one-third of them, and that of the 84 Nobel Prizes won by researchers working at universities and research institutes in the United Kingdom, immigrants won 32 (38.1%) of them (p.76).

It is useful to note that at least, three immigrants to the United States won Nobel Prizes in the fall of 2015 but are not included in this study. Angus Deaton, born in Scotland, UK (economics, employed at Princeton University, New Jersey); William C. Campbell, born in Ireland (physiology or medicine, employed at Drew University, Madison, New Jersey);and Aziz Sancar, born in Turkey (Chemistry, employed at the University of North Carolina, Chapel Hill) ("Nobel Prizes 2015," 2015).

This study examines the background of those naturalized immigrants recognized by the Carnegie Corporation of New York as "Great Immigrants" from 2006 to 2015. It begins by (re)conceptualizing the 'brain drain' phenomenon as competition. The following methodology section explains how the data for this study were collected or compiled, after which the results or findings are explained. Finally, a discussion section is presented. We now turn to the concept of the "brain drain."

CHAPTER TWO

(RE)CONCEPTUALIZING THE BRAIN DRAIN PHENOMENON AS COMPETITION

Many of these "Pride of America" immigrants could have accomplished their feats for their own ancestral lands or nations of citizenship. Instead, circumstances resulted in them doing so for the United States, thereby making it, in the opinion of many, the world's leading nation in terms of science and technology, arts and entertainment, sports, religious tolerance, and so on. Albert Einstein's emigration was America's gain but a loss to Germany, Switzerland, and Asia because he had German and Swiss citizenship and blood ancestry or heritage from Israel, Western Asia. Daniel C. Tsui's emigration was America's gain but China's loss, for he won the Nobel Prize in Physics in 1998 as an American citizen, not a citizen of his ancestral land.

Both Einstein's and Tsui's becoming American citizens can be explained by the brain drain phenomenon, but in two slightly different dimensions. Einstein left Germany not because it was underdeveloped compared with other European nations or the United States and Canada, but because of ethnic or racial discrimination or prejudice. Tsu, on the other hand, emigrated as a result of what much of the "brain drain" literature now focuses on: the movement of talented or highly skilled individuals from developing nations to developed nations (Gaulé & Piacentini, 2013; Han et al., 2015; Kaba, 2011; Kim et al., 2011; Lee & Skop, 2010; Robinoff, 2005; Shachar, 2011; Shachar & Hirschl, 2013). As Han et al. (2015) note of skilled workers from developing countries emigrating to developed countries since the 1960s, the "…literature is concerned with the economic and development impact caused by this migration, which early models showed to be a net negative for the sending country and a net positive for the receiving country" (p.2).

There now appears to be a third dimension to this phenomenon: (1) The emigration of highly talented or skilled and wealthy individuals from developed nations, nations on the verge of being categorized as developed to other developed nations, or even to developing nations;

(2) Immigrants in developed nations returning to their home nations or regions to start a business or take various employment positions; (3) and skilled immigrants in developed nations moving between home countries and their new wealthy nations of citizenship – a reverse brain drain or "brain circulation". Many of these skilled emigrants are choosing to relocate in certain geographic areas or academic or technological locations, such as universities and Silicon Valley – "brain clusters." While there is some evidence that the United States is losing a significant number of its talented citizens or residents to other nations or regions of the world, the data in this study shows that it continues to get the lion's share of this new form of skilled international migration. (Campanella, 2015; Gaulé & Piacentini, 2013; Han et al., 2015; Kerr & Lincoln, 2010; Kim et al., 2011; Lee & Skop, 2010; No & Walsh, 2010; Ornstein, 2015; Rodriguez, 2014; Saxenian, 2002; Shachar, 2011; Shachar & Hirschl, 2013; Tiech, 2014; Wadhwa, 2009).

Campanella (2015) laments the challenges that European nations, including the wealthiest ones in the European Union (EU) are facing, in terms of losing their brightest minds to North America, Australia, South America, and Africa. The great demand for highly skilled individuals during a period when more nations are opening their borders to them means that no government or nation can retain their brightest stars. Political crisis, inadequate investments in technology or institutional shortcomings have resulted in a continuous brain drain, affecting Europe from the 1940s to the present. As Campanella (2015) notes:

> In this sense, Europe is a case in point. For more than half a century, bright academics, ambitious entrepreneurs, and visionary scientists have defeated the conservatism of Europe by crossing the Atlantic Ocean in search of vibrant university environments and rewarding professional opportunities. These emigrants are not only Europe's most skilled workers but, according to several metrics, also the most gifted in their respective fields globally, with their "quality"— expressed in terms of educational and professional backgrounds— having significantly increased over time. In short, this is the brain drain of "la creme de la creme." To make matters worse, Europe's outflows of human capital have rarely been compensated by adequate inflows of equally skilled foreign talents from either developed or developing economies (pp.195-196).

According to Campanella (2015), fewer skilled Americans are relocating to Europe; however, substantial numbers of skilled Europeans are relocating to the United States. In addition, the United States gets the brightest minds relocating from developing countries. "By 2020, Europe's digital sector alone will experience a shortage [of] 900,000 professionals, whereas the dynamic German economy will need 1 million skilled workers in science, technology, engineering, and mathematics (STEM)" (p.196). The United Kingdom, Germany, Greece, Ireland, and Portugal are reported to be impacted by this brain drain. Ten percent of Greek academics are reported to be working primarily in the United Kingdom or the United States. A reported 100,000 skilled Portuguese professionals left their country in 2011 to seek jobs abroad, partly because their own prime minister encouraged them to do so. By 2009, 18% of German researchers and 16% of Irish doctorate degree holders had emigrated to the other side of the Atlantic Ocean, especially the United States and Canada. As for the United Kingdom, the term "brain drain" was developed in the 1960s to explain the loss of its citizens to the United States and Canada: "In the wake of a heated public debate, an article in the Evening Standard coined the term 'brain drain' for the first time." The United Kingdom not only experiences a primary brain drain, but also a secondary brain drain, whereby skilled immigrants leave the United Kingdom for other developed nations. From 1967 to 1986, a quarter of the Nobel Prize winners in scientific fields in the United Kingdom were immigrants. However, from 1987 to 2006, that "...figure dropped to zero" (Campanella, 2015, pp.198-202).

The EU as a whole or individual EU nations have not managed to develop policies that would result in a reverse brain drain or a brain circulation such as those "... provided by Indian and Israeli engineers, who have contributed to the establishment of thriving information technology industries after having returned to their countries of origin. However, in Europe, when talents depart they rarely return, or they do so at the end of their careers, when they are less likely to positively influence the system." For example, from 1996 to 2011, while 42,000 European scientists emigrated to the United States, Canada and Australia, only 31,000 such skilled professionals emigrated from those nations to Europe. In 2000, the EU hosted 20% of skilled immigrants from developing nations, only to lose 75% of them who relocated to the United States and Australia (Campanella, 2015, pp.202-203). It is reported that 25% of all high-tech companies in Silicon Valley were founded by immigrant entrepreneurs from 1995 to 2005, and that of the top 10 patent-producing universities in the United States in 2011, 76% of the patents awarded to them included at least one immigrant innovator. Also, 27% of the American workforce is comprised of high-skilled foreign-born individuals with a doctorate degree, and they are heavily concentrated in high skill professions, including 43% of medical scientists and 25% of physicists (Shachar & Hirschl, 2013, p.99; also see Kerr & Lincoln, 2010, pp.474 & 479; No & Walsh, 2010, p.290; Shkumatava, 2014, p.56).

Shachar and Hirschl (2013) discussed the efforts of many developed and advanced developing nations to recruit skilled or talented individuals from different fields (e.g., professional athletes and scientists) from abroad. Among the nations examined are members of the EU (e.g., Germany and the United Kingdom), the United States, Australia, Canada, China, New Zealand, Singapore, Taiwan, and South Korea. Among the incentives offered is expedited citizenship. China, for example, is reported to be very actively recruiting skilled professionals: "As part of its One-Thousand-Talent program, China is also aggressively using financial, taxation, and membership perks to attract high-caliber international scholars and returning Chinese citizens to lead key laboratories, projects and disciplines in China" (Shachar & Hirschl, 2013, p.84). While discussing the reverse brain drain or brain circulation of international students in developed countries going home after earning their terminal or advanced higher education degrees, Han et al. (2015) point out that the immigrants' remittances, the spillover of skills to other workers, and the spread of technologies from advanced countries to developing countries are part of this new phenomenon. They add "In particular, advancements in information technology and the increasing interconnectedness of a globalized economy have created new opportunities for migrants to quickly push innovations back to their home countries" (p.2). Han et al. (2015) present a table entitled "Table 1. List of programs, by country, that promote the return of Science, Technology, Engineering, and Mathematics (STEM) talent back to their home country" (pp.4-5). Wadhwa (2009) notes of an Indian entrepreneur who hired "100 returnee scientists" in 2006 alone. We also found evidence of startup activity in the pharmaceutical industry, with Indian startups relying on research or executive teams with experience working for major U.S. drug companies." American companies such as IBM, Microsoft, Cisco, and General Electric are among those companies based overseas, including in India, that are luring highly skilled immigrants in the United States to return home to work (pp. 49-50; also see Saxenian, 2002). As Shkumatava (2014) notes:

> The United States today is in a worldwide competition for the best scientific and engineering talent. Countries that were minor players in science and technology a few years ago are rapidly entering the major leagues and actively pursuing scientific and technical talent in the global marketplace. The advent of rapid and inexpensive global communication and air travel that is within easy reach of researchers in many countries have fostered the growth of global networks of collaboration and are changing the way research is done (p.56).

The year of birth and previous nationality data of the "Pride of America" honorees in Tables 4 and 5 below also show that many of them could have stayed home or gone back home because they became adults at a time when their countries of citizenship were already developed. Therefore, there should have been no real reason for them to emigrate. These nations include Canada, Australia, the United Kingdom, Germany, Italy, Spain, Switzerland, France, Japan, Ireland, Norway, South Korea, and Taiwan. From 2008-2014, 104,189 temporary visa holders in the United States earned doctorate degrees, and 71.1% of them said they intended to remain in the country, 42% out of 562 for Singapore, 63% out of 4,805 for Taiwan, 63.5% out of 840 for France, 58% out of 1,401 for Germany, 61.4% out of 1,040 for Italy, 56.3% out of 3,330 for Canada, 88.2% out of 1,802 for Iran, and 60.7% out of 634 for Israel ("Table 53. Doctorate Recipients with temporary visas," 2014).

Finally, American government policies are causing relatively wealthy Americans to give up their citizenship (Manieri, 2015; Newlove, 2016; Ross, 2015; Wood, 2015). Record numbers of Americans have been doing so, and the numbers have increased annually for the past several years. This is due partly to a U.S. government law called Fatca (the Foreign Account Tax Compliance Act), which requires every American citizen, regardless of where they reside, to file federal taxes. The law was passed in 2012 and went into full effect in 2013 to prevent tax evasion (Newlove, 2016; Ross 2015). Other factors have also been cited, including political. According to Ross (2015), increasing numbers of American citizens give up their citizenship "... each year than leave the United States and ask for political asylum.... All told, 3,415 Americans renounced their citizenship for what were likely financial reasons – a record figure. Just 188 citizens sought asylum in another country." In 2011, 1,781 Americans renounced their citizenship, 932 in 2012, 2,999 in 2013, 3,415 in 2014, and 4,279 in 2015. Only the United States and Eritrea are reported to have such a law (Ross, 2015; Newlove, 2016).

CHAPTER THREE

METHODOLOGY, DATA AVAILABILITY, RELIABILITY, AND LIMITATIONS OF THIS STUDY

The decision to conduct this study was in June 2015, when I read news stories of the 2015 group of Carnegie Corporation's great immigrants. I then found out that the program had begun with its first group of honorees in 2006. I decided to compile information, as provided on the program's website (http://greatimmigrants.carnegie.org/), on all of the honorees from 2006 to 2015. Table A1, which is a result of that effort; include the names of each honoree, previous citizenship or nationality, and profession. I then created a primary table with the following variables: sex/gender, race, date of birth(with a separate focus on month and year of birth), previous citizenship or nationality, geographic/regional location of previous country of citizenship, educational attainment (highest/terminal higher education degree earned), academic major, year of graduation, academic institution of earned degree, U.S. state and nation of academic institution, U.S. geographic region and world region of academic institution, and net worth.

On its website, the Carnegie Corporation presents the previous nationality or country of citizenship for 407 of the 408 honorees. The one remaining honoree had two previous nationalities or citizenships (Italy and Egypt) listed. I discovered that he originally had Egyptian citizenship, noted or highlighted his Egyptian ancestry in a number of his writings, and identifies more with his Egyptian heritage. As a result, only his Egyptian citizenship is utilized in this study. The Carnegie Corporation wrongly listed one honoree of Haitian ancestry who was born in the Democratic Republic of Congo as an Iranian. In this study, he is listed as Haitian American because that is how he identifies himself and how almost everyone identifies him (based on my own research).

For the geographic region of previous country of citizenship or nationality, the United Nations statistics division of the regional breakdowns or classifications of the world are utilized (http://unstats.un.org/unsd/methods/m49/m49regin.htm) For the regional breakdown of the United States (Midwest, Northeast, South, and West), the United States Census classification is utilized (see Kaba, 2015, p.31).

For the race variable, I utilize the official American government's racial/ethnic categorization. For example, in the United States, anyone with Black African ancestry is categorized as Black. Arabs (who are not Black) from nations in North Africa or Western Asia; people from Israel, Iran, Afghanistan, and anyone with European Caucasian ancestry are all categorized as White. People from East Asia, South Asia (e.g., Bangladesh, India, and Pakistan), and Southeast Asia are all categorized as Asian. However, if a person categorized in the United States as Asian were to have a child with a person categorized as White, then that child is categorized as White. One male honoree is half-Indian (South Asia) and half-European American; he is categorized as White in this study. There are two female honorees, each having a Southeast Asian parent, and another parent with various European Caucasian or White ancestries; they are therefore categorized as White in this study (Gans, 2012; Kaba, 2015, pp.120-121; "Standards for the Classification of Federal Data on Race and Ethnicity," 1995; Yancey 2003). Pertaining to this country's racial and ethnic categorization of people, the United States Office of Management and Budget points out that: "The term 'Black' in Directive No. 15 refers to a person having origins in any of the Black racial groups of Africa." Explaining who belongs to the White category: "In Directive No. 15, the 'White' category includes persons having origins in any of the original peoples of Europe, North Africa, or the Middle East" ("Standards for the Classification of Federal Data on Race and Ethnicity," 1995; Kaba, 2015, pp.120-121).

For the educational attainment data, I decided to utilize earned highest or terminal college or higher education degrees. If an honoree had earned a bachelor's degree or higher, I used the highest degree. If an honoree had earned any number of master's degrees only, I counted all of them. If an honoree had earned a master's and a JD, I counted both of them. If an honoree had earned a master's and a doctorate (such as Ph.D. or Ed.D.), I counted only the doctorate; I counted a doctorate and an MD (Doctor of Medicine), or a doctorate and a JD (Juris Doctor).

For the net worth data, I found figures for 122 (29.9%) of the 408 honorees: 87 men and 35 women. The vast majority of these data are from two key sources that are widely used by the public: (1) the website of *Forbes Magazine* for almost all of the billionaires and (2) the website called celebritynetworth.com. Other sources utilized are newspapers, magazines, books, and so on. The data from the two key sources are from November 14-18, 2015. The billionaire data from *Forbes Magazine* tend to fluctuate based on the financial markets – a figure today might not be the same a week later. There is a female honoree (Marie-Josée Kravis), whose net worth was half of her husband's network listed on *Forbes Magazine*. Another female honoree's (Elaine Chao) net worth was also half of her husband's net worth reported in newspapers. The reason is that in the United States, a married spouse can inherit half or all of her or his spouse's estate or is legally entitled to up to half of the estate in a divorce. The figure for Paul Merage is half of what is listed for him and his brother on Forbes' list of billionaires. I included the web url or link in the table to each figure for all of the 122 honorees for whom data were available.

In terms of how valid or reliable these data are, I spent a substantial amount of time carefully searching public information on the web pertaining to each honoree: dissertations, their work or personal websites, books, newspaper/magazine articles about them, Wikipedia entries, radio and television interviews, and so on. I did not contact any honoree to request any of his or her personal information. I checked and rechecked all of the data I compiled to ensure consistency. Although there is no guarantee that all of these data are accurate, it is important to examine what was found and share it with the public in order to acquire a better understanding of these distinguished honorees' experiences.

CHAPTER FOUR

FINDINGS/RESULTS AND ANALYSIS

Gender/Sex

Regardless of geographic location, race, ethnicity, or religion, men tend be honored or recognized more than their female counterparts. This phenomenon is observed in academia, business, politics, and many other professions (Black and Rothman, 1998; Caprino, 2011; "The FP Top Global Thinkers," 2011; Hartlet et al., 2016, p.127; Kaba, 2012, p.7, 2015, 2016). This study shows a continuation of that trend. According to Table 1, of the 408 combined honorees from 2006-2015, men accounted for 289 (70.8%) and women accounted for 119 (29.2%).

Table 1. Carnegie Corporation of New York's "Pride of America" Honorees, by Sex: 2006-2015
N=408

Sex	Number	%
Men	289	70.8
Women	119	29.2
Total	408	100.0

Source: Compiled and computed from June 24, 2015 to January 6, 2016, based on data from: "Great Immigrants: The Pride of America". Carnegie Corporation of New York. http://greatimmigrants.carnegie.org/pride-america/.

Racial Background of "Pride of America" Honorees, 2006-2015

As discussed in the methodology section, the racial classifications of immigrants living in the United States differ from such classifications in other societies or countries. For example, an Arab, Afghan, Israeli, Iranian, or Turk is officially categorized as White, whereas a Black person from anywhere in the world is categorized as Black. Individuals who are half-Asian and half-European are categorized as White. Table 2 presents the racial breakdown of all 408 honorees. According to Table 2, Whites accounted for the majority 271 (66.4%); Asians, 102 (25%); and Blacks, 34 (8.3%). There was one American Indian (0.2%).

The data show that Asians are overrepresented in this study even with the country's unique racial categorization. In 2014, there were 12.8 million Asians in the United States, with 59% of them representing naturalized citizens, compared with 47% of all immigrants (or 20 million out of 42.4 million foreign-born population) (Zong and Batalova, 2016, January 6; Zong and Batalova, 2016, April 14). Black naturalized citizens, on the other hand, account for 2.05 million (10.6%) of the 19.43 million total naturalized citizens in the United States in 2013. Fifty-four percent of the 3.793 million Black immigrants in the United States (out of 41.341 million foreign-born population) were citizens in 2013 (Compiled and computed from Anderson, 2015, p.9). This data show that while Black immigrants as a group are the least accepted into the United States, a higher proportion of them are naturalized citizens, compared with all immigrants. However, their proportion in Table 2 is lower than their proportion among all naturalized immigrants.

According to Table 2, based on sex or gender, White men accounted for 187 (45.8%, but 64.7% of all men) of all honorees; Asian men, 71 (17.4%, but 24.6% of all men); Black men, 30 (7.4%, but 10.4% of all men); and the one American Indian man (0.3% of all men). There are 84 White women (20.5% of total, but 70.6% of all women); Asian women, 31 (7.6% or total, but 26% of all women); and Black women, 4 (1% of total, but 3.4% of all women) (Table 2).

Table 2. Carnegie Corporation of New York's "Pride of America" Honorees, by Race and Sex: 2006-2015
N=408

Category	All Honorees	%	Men	% of Total	% of Men	Women	% of Total	% of Women
Asian	102	25	71	17.4	24.6	31	7.6	26
Black	34	8.3	30	7.4	10.4	4	1.0	3.4
American Indian	1	0.2	1	0.2	0.3	0	0	0
White	271	66.4	187	45.8	64.7	84	20.5	70.6
Total	408	100	289	70.8	100	119	29.2	100

Source: Compiled and computed from June 24, 2015 to January 6, 2016, based on data from: "Great Immigrants: The Pride of America". Carnegie Corporation of New York. http://greatimmigrants.carnegie.org /pride-america/.

Month of Birth of Carnegie Corporation of New York's "Pride of America" Honorees, by Race and Sex, 2006-2015

Scholars have studied month of birth data from various perspectives, including academic attainment, sports, health status, business leadership, longevity, and so on. These studies have shown some differences and similarities of individuals born in a particular month or season (Abel & Kruger, 2010; Delorme et al., 2010; Du et al., 2012; Edgar & O'Donoghue, 2005; Martin et. al., 2009; Melina, 2010). Abel and Kruger (2010) note that an increasing body of research studies shows that: "…the month of birth may be related to longevity" (p.757). Du et al. (2012) find in their study of corporate CEOs in the United States that "…individuals born in June and July have a significantly lower chance of becoming a CEO than those born in other months" (p.660).

The month of birth data in this study were collected to observe whether there are any similarities among the honorees, since all of them were born abroad, and to determine whether there are any similarities between them as a group and any available data of people born in the United States. According to Table 3, month of birth data are available for 335 (82.1%) of the 408 honorees: 37 (11.1%) were born in January, 33 (9.9%) in May, 31 (9.3%) in August, and 29 (8.7%) in November. For men, of the 242 (72.2% of 335 total) with month of birth data, 31 (12.8%) were born in January, 26 (10.7%) in May, 23 (9.5%) in November, and 22 (9.1%) in December. For women, of the 93 (27.8% of 335 total) honorees with month of birth data, 14 (15.1%) were born in August, 11 (11.8%) in October, and 10 (10.8%) in September.

Among the various racial groups, 24 (10.3%) of 233 Whites were born in May, 22 (9.4%) in January, and 21 (9%) in March. Of 166 (49.6% of 335 total) White men, 20 (12%) were born in May, 18 (10.8%) in January, 16 (9.6%) in July, and 15 (9%) each in March and June. Of 67 (20% of 335 total) White women, 10 (14.9%) were born in August and 9 (13.4%) each in September and October. Of 73 (21.8% of 335 total) Asians, 10 (13.7%) were born in August and 9 (12.3%) each in January, October, and November. Of 51 Asian males (15.2% of 335 total), 8 (15.7%) were born in January, 7 (13.7%) in October, and 6 (11.8%) in August. Of 22 (6.6% of 335 total) Asian women, 4 (18.2%) each were born in August and November and 3 (13.6%) in June. Of 28

(8.4% of 335 total) Blacks, 6 (21.4%) were born in January, 4 (14.3%) in May, and 3 (10.7%) each in March, April, November, and December. Of 24 (7.2% of 335) Black men, 5 (20.8%) were born in January and 3 (12.5%) each in March, April, May, November, and December. Of 4 Black women, each (25%) was born in January, February, May, and July. Finally, the American Indian (AI) man was born in December (Table 3).

Table 3. Month of Birth of Carnegie Corporation of New York's "Pride of America" Honorees, by Race and Sex, 2006-2015 N=335

Month	All #	%	Men	%	Women	%	White	%	Men	%	Women	%	Asian	%	Men	%	Women	%	Black	%	Men	%	Women	%	AI Man	%
January	37	11.1	31	12.8	6	6.5	22	9.4	18	10.8	4	6.0	9	12.3	8	15.7	1	4.5	6	21.4	5	20.8	1	25.0		
February	24	7.2	17	7.0	7	7.5	17	7.3	12	7.2	5	7.5	6	8.2	5	9.8	1	4.5	1	3.6			1	25.0		
March	27	8.1	20	8.3	7	7.5	21	9.0	15	9.0	6	9.0	3	4.1	2	3.9	1	4.5	3	10.7	3	12.5				
April	25	7.5	18	7.4	7	7.5	19	8.2	13	7.8	6	9.0	3	4.1	2	3.9	1	4.5	3	10.7	3	12.5				
May	33	9.9	26	10.7	7	7.5	24	10.3	20	12.0	4	6.0	5	6.8	3	5.9	2	9.1	4	14.3	3	12.5	1	25.0		
June	25	7.5	19	7.9	6	6.5	18	7.7	15	9.0	3	4.5	5	6.8	2	3.9	3	13.6	2	7.1	2	8.3				
July	25	7.5	19	7.9	6	6.5	20	8.6	16	9.6	4	6.0	4	5.5	3	5.9	1	4.5	1	3.6			1	25.0		
August	31	9.3	17	7.0	14	15.1	20	8.6	10	6.0	10	14.9	10	13.7	6	11.8	4	18.2	1	3.6	1	4.2				
September	23	6.9	13	5.4	10	10.8	18	7.7	9	5.4	9	13.4	5	6.8	4	7.8	1	4.5								
October	28	8.4	17	7.0	11	11.8	18	7.7	9	5.4	9	13.4	9	12.3	7	13.7	2	9.1	1	3.6	1	4.2				
November	29	8.7	23	9.5	6	6.5	17	7.3	15	9.0	2	3.0	9	12.3	5	9.8	4	18.2	3	10.7	3	12.5				
December	28	8.4	22	9.1	6	6.5	19	8.2	14	8.4	5	7.5	5	6.8	4	7.8	1	4.5	3	10.7	3	12.5			1	10
Total	335	100	##	100	93	100	233	100	166	100	67	100	73	100	51	100	22	100	28	100	24	100	4	100	1	10

Source: Compiled and computed from June 24, 2015, to January 6, 2016, based on data from: "Great Immigrants: The Pride of America". Carnegie Corporation of New York. http://greatimmigrants.carnegie.org/pride-america/.

Note: AI= American Indian

Year of Birth of Carnegie Corporation of New York's "Pride of America" Honorees, by Race and Sex, 2006-2015

The year of birth of the "Pride of America" honorees in this study could be found useful by readers in many ways. It gives an overall historical perspective of the honorees as a whole, shows that the emigration of talented individuals to this country is a continuous process, and presents a perspective on the major issues across the world around the times when they were born. The year of birth data also illustrate that a significant number of White honorees born in Europe or Australia could have remained or returned to their home countries because those nations were relatively economically successful while those honorees were in their 20s, 30s, or 40s. Table 4 shows that the year of birth data are available for 390 (95.6%) of the 408 honorees. Of the 390 honorees (born in 70 different years from 1879 to 1989), for whom year of birth data are available, double figure numbers of them were born in nine different years, starting in 1947: 14 (3.6%) each in 1951 and 1955; 12 (3.1%) each in 1949, 1950, 1952, 1956, and 1968; 11 (2.8%) in 1959; and 10 (2.6%) in 1947. Twenty-three (5.9%) of them were born from 1975 to 1989, and 45 (11.5%) of them were born from 1879 to 1929.

Thirteen men (3.3%) were born in 1951 and 10 men (2.6%) in 1952. Eight women (2.1%) were born in 1955 and 5 women (1.3%) each in 1956, 1959, and 1961. Twelve Whites (3.1%) were born in 1951 and 10 Whites (2.6%) in 1950: 11 White men (2.8%) were born in 1951, 8 (2.1%) in 1946, and 7 (1.8%) in 1952; 5 White women (1.3%) were born in 1959 and 4 (1%) each in 1950, 1955, 1956, and 1961. Six Asians (1.5%) were born in 1955, 1967, and 1974: Five Asian men (1.3%) were born in 1967, 4 (1%) in 1974, and 3 (0.8%) each in 1948, 1952, 1954, 1955, 1956, and 1970; 3 Asian women (0.8%) each in 1947 and 1955, and 2 (0.5%) each in 1938, 1957, 1958, 1962, and 1974. Finally, 3 Blacks (0.8%) each were born in 1949, 1966, and 1975, and 2 (0.5%) each in 1939, 1955, 1968, 1980, and 1985: 3 Black men (0.8%) each in 1966 and 1975, and 2 (0.5%) each in 1939, 1949, 1968, and 1980; 1 Black woman (0.26%) each in 1949, 1955, 1969, and 1985 (Table 4).

Table 4. Year of Birth of Carnegie Corporation of New York's "Pride of America" Honorees, by Race and Sex, 2006-2015
n=390 honorees born in 70 different years from 1879 to 1989.

Year	All #	%	Men	%	Women	%	White	%	Men	%	Women	%	Asian	%	Men	%	Women	%	Black	%	Men	%	Women	%
1879	1	0.3	1	0.4			1	0.4	1	0.6														
1911	1	0.3			1	1.0	1	0.4			1	1.3												
1914	1	0.3	1	0.4			1	0.4	1	0.6														
1915	1	0.3	1	0.4			1	0.4	1	0.6														
1917	1	0.3	1	0.4				0.0					1	1.0	1	1.4								
1920	4	1.0	3	1.1	1	1.0	3	1.2	2	1.1	1	1.3	1	1.0	1	1.4								
1921	2	0.5	2	0.7			1	0.4	1	0.6			1	1.0	1	1.4								
1922	3	0.8	3	1.1			1	0.4	1	0.6			2	2.1	2	2.9								
1923	4	1.0	4	1.4			3	1.2	3	1.7				0.0										
1924	6	1.5	4	1.4	2	2.0	6	2.3	4	2.2	2	2.6												
1925	3	0.8	2	0.7	1	1.0	3	1.2	2	1.1	1	1.3												
1926	4	1.0	4	1.4			2	0.8	2	1.1			2	2.1	2	2.9								
1927	2	0.5	1	0.4	1	1.0	2	0.8	1	0.6	1	1.3												
1928	6	1.5	6	2.1			5	1.9	5	2.8			1	1.0	1	1.4								
1929	6	1.5	6	2.1			6	2.3	6	3.3														
1930	6	1.5	4	1.4	2	2.0	5	1.9	3	1.7	2	2.6												
1931	6	1.5	5	1.8	1	1.0	6	2.3	5	2.8	1	1.3												
1932	4	1.0	4	1.4			4	1.6	4	2.2														
1933	6	1.5	4	1.4	2	2.0	4	1.6	3	1.7	1	1.3	2	2.1	1	1.4	1	3.6						
1934	4	1.0	2	0.7	2	2.0	3	1.2	1	0.6	2	2.6	1	1.0	1	1.4								
1935	4	1.0	4	1.4			4	1.6	4	2.2														
1936	4	1.0	4	1.4			4	1.6	4	2.2														
1937	4	1.0	3	1.1	1	1.0	4	1.6	3	1.7	1	1.3												
1938	8	2.1	4	1.4	4	4.0	5	1.9	3	1.7	2	2.6	3	3.1	1	1.4	2	7.1						
1939	5	1.3	3	1.1	2	2.0	2	0.8			2	2.6	1	1.0	1	1.4			2	6.1	2	6.9		
1940	5	1.3	5	1.8			4	1.6	4	2.2			1	1.0	1	1.4								

Table 4 continues…

Year	All #	%	Men	%	Women	%	White	%	Men	%	Women	%	Asian	%	Men	%	Women	%	Black	%	Men	%	Women	%
1941	7	1.8	4	1.4	3	3.0	7	2.7	4	2.2	3	3.8												
1942	3	0.8	1	0.4	2	2.0	2	0.8	1	0.6	1	1.3	1	1.0					1	3.6				
1943	3	0.8	3	1.1			3	1.2	3	1.7														
1944	6	1.5	5	1.8	1	1.0	4	1.6	4	2.2			2	2.1	1	1.4			1	3.6				
1945	6	1.5	5	1.8	1	1.0	3	1.2	2	1.1	1	1.3	2	2.1	2	2.9			1	3.0	1	3.4		
1946	9	2.3	9	3.2			8	3.1	8	4.4			1	1.0	1	1.4								
1947	10	2.6	6	2.1	4	4.0	5	1.9	4	2.2	1	1.3	5	5.2	2	2.9	3	10.7						
1948	7	1.8	6	2.1	1	1.0	4	1.6	3	1.7	1	1.3	3	3.1	3	4.3								
1949	12	3.1	7	2.5	5	5.0	7	2.7	4	2.2	3	3.8	2	2.1	1	1.4	1	3.6	3	9.1	2	6.9	1	25.0
1950	12	3.1	8	2.9	4	4.0	10	3.9	6	3.3	4	5.1	1	1.0	1	1.4			1	3.0	1	3.4		
1951	14	3.6	13	4.6	1	1.0	12	4.7	11	6.1	1	1.3	2	2.1	2	2.9								
1952	12	3.1	10	3.6	2	2.0	9	3.5	7	3.9	2	2.6	3	3.1	3	4.3								
1953	6	1.5	5	1.8	1	1.0	4	1.6	4	2.2			2	2.1	1	1.4	1	3.6						
1954	4	1.0	4	1.4			1	0.4	1	0.6			3	3.1	3	4.3								
1955	14	3.6	6	2.1	8	8.0	6	2.3	2	1.1	4	5.1	6	6.2	3	4.3	3	10.7	2	6.1	1	3.4	1	25.0
1956	12	3.1	7	2.5	5	5.0	8	3.1	4	2.2	4	5.1	4	4.1	3	4.3	1	3.6						
1957	8	2.1	4	1.4	4	4.0	3	1.2	1	0.6	2	2.6	4	4.1	2	2.9	2	7.1	1	3.0	1			
1958	7	1.8	4	1.4	3	3.0	4	1.6	3	1.7	1	1.3	2	2.1			2	7.1	1	3.0	1	3.4		
1959	11	2.8	6	2.1	5	5.0	9	3.5	4	2.2	5	6.4	2	2.1	2	2.9								
1960	4	1.0	3	1.1	1	1.0	4	1.6	3	1.7	1	1.3												
1961	8	2.1	3	1.1	5	5.0	6	2.3	2	1.1	4	5.1	2	2.1	1	1.4	1	3.6						
1962	8	2.1	6	2.1	2	2.0	4	1.6	4	2.2			3	3.1	1	1.4	2	7.1	1	3.0	1	3.4		
1963	4	1.0	3	1.1	1	1.0	2	0.8	1	0.6	1	1.3	1	1.0	1	1.4			1	3.0	1	3.4		
1964	6	1.5	5	1.8	1	1.0	4	1.6	3	1.7	1	1.3	1	1.0	1	1.4			1	3.0	1	3.4		
1965	7	1.8	4	1.4	3	3.0	5	1.9	3	1.7	2	2.6	2	2.1	1	1.4	1	3.6						
1966	7	1.8	4	1.4	3	3.0	2	0.8			2	2.6	2	2.1	1	1.4	1	3.6	3	9.1	3	10.3		
1967	9	2.3	8	2.9	1	1.0	2	0.8	2	1.1			6	6.2	5	7.2	1	3.6	1	3.0	1	3.4		
1968	12	3.1	10	3.6	2	2.0	7	2.7	6	3.3	1	1.3	3	3.1	2	2.9	1	3.6	2	6.1	2	6.9		

Table 4 continues…

All Years	#	%	Men	%	Women	%	White	%	Men	%	Women	%	Asian	%	Men	%	Women	%	Black	%	Men	%	Women	%
1969	6	1.5	4	1.4	2	2.0	3	1.2	3	1.7			2	2.1	1	1.4	1	3.6	1	3.0			1	25.0
1970	6	1.5	5	1.8	1	1.0	2	0.8	1	0.6	1	1.3	3	3.1	3	4.3			1	3.0	1	3.4		
1971	4	1.0	2	0.7	2	2.0	3	1.2	1	0.6	2	2.6							1	3.0	1	3.4		
1972	8	2.1	7	2.5	1	1.0	6	2.3	5	2.8	1	1.3	2	2.1	2	2.9								
1973	5	1.3	3	1.1	2	2.0	4	1.6	2	1.1	2	2.6	1	1.0	1	1.4								
1974	9	2.3	7	2.5	2	2.0	2	0.8	2	1.1			6	6.2	4	5.8	2	7.1	1	3.0	1	3.4		
1975	8	2.1	5	1.8	3	3.0	5	1.9	2	1.1	3	3.8							3	9.1	3	10.3		
1976	1	0.3			1	1.0	1	0.4			1	1.3												
1978	3	0.8	2	0.7	1	1.0	1	0.4			1	1.3	1	1.0	1	1.4			1	3.0	1	3.4		
1980	2	0.5	2	0.7				0.0											2	6.1	2	6.9		
1981	2	0.5	1	0.4	1	1.0	1	0.4			1	1.3							1	3.0	1	3.4		
1982	1	0.3			1	1.0	1	0.4			1	1.3												
1983	1	0.3			1	1.0	1	0.4			1	1.3												
1985	2	0.5	1	0.4	1	1.0		0.0											2	6.1	1	3.4	1	25.
1986	1	0.3			1	1.0	1	0.4			1	1.3												
1989	2	0.5	1	0.4	1	1.0	1	0.4			1	1.3	1	1.0	1	1.4								
Total	390	100.0	280	100.0	110	110.0	258	100.0	180	100.0	78	100.0	97	100.0	69	100.0	28	100.0	33	100.0	29	100.0	4	100

Source: Compiled and computed from June 24, 2015, to January 6, 2016, based on data from: "Great Immigrants: The Pride of America". Carnegie Corporation of New York. http://greatimmigrants.carnegie.org/pride-america/.

Previous Nationality/Citizenship of Carnegie Corporation of New York's "Pride of America" Honorees, by Race and Sex, 2006-2015

Part of the greatness of the United States can be found in the significant, to substantial numbers and proportions of people from various racial, ethnic, or ancestry groups from all over the world who live there. This racial, ethnic, and cultural diversity is primarily the result of the different dimensions of the brain drain discussed above (Anderson, 2015; Bankston III., 2007; Blank, 2014; Bozorgmehr & Douglas, 2011; Donato et al., 2007; Greenwood & Ward, 2015; Jaret & Kolozsvari, 2011; Li & Skop, 2010; Michopoulos, 2013; "People Reporting Ancestry," 2015; Rubinoff, 2005; Scott, 2005; Timberlake & Williams, 2012). The United States also has one of the world's largest immigrant populations. For example, in 2013, it had 41.341 million immigrants, with naturalized citizens accounting for 47% (Anderson, 2015, p.9) of them. By 2016, there were at least 238 countries and geographic entities in the world, according to the 2016 CIA World Factbook. The diversity of nations represented in this study illustrates how open the United States has been, especially from the mid-1960s to the present.

Table 5 shows that these 408 "Pride of America" naturalized honorees are from 87 different nations/geographic entities. The nations with 10 or more honorees are India, 29 (7.1%); China, 28 (6.9%); England, UK, 22 (5.4%); Canada and Germany each, 20 (4.9%); Iran, 18 (4.4%); Cuba, 17 (4.2%); Mexico, 14 (3.4%) and Israel and Russia each, 13 (3.2%). It is useful to note that if the 1 (0.2%) honoree from Hong Kong is added to China's 28, both China and India would be tied at 29. If the 7 (1.7%) honorees from Taiwan were added to China, its total would be 36 (8.8%). On the other hand, if the honorees from nations that formed India before World War II were added together, their total would be 35 (8.6%): India, 29; Bangladesh, 1 (0.2%); and Pakistan, 5 (1.2%). Also, if the 3 (0.7%) honorees from Scotland, UK, were added to England's 22, their total would be 25 (6.1%).

Among men, the following nations/geographic entities have 10 or more honorees: India, 24 (5.8% of the total 408 honorees); China, 21 (5.1%); England, UK, 17 (4.2%); Canada, 16 (3.9%); Germany, 14 (3.4%); and Israel and Iran each, 10 (2.5%). Among women, the following nations/geographic entities have 5 or more honorees: Cuba and Iran each, 8 (2% of the total 408 honorees); China and Mexico each, 7 (1.7%); Germany, 6 (1.5%); and England, UK, and India each, 5 (1.2%).

Among racial groups, the following nations/geographic entities have 10 or more White honorees: Canada and England, UK, each, 19 (4.7% of the total 408 honorees); Germany, 20 (4.9%); Iran, 18 (4.4%); Cuba, 17 (4.2%); Mexico, 14 (3.4%); and Israel and Russia each, 13 (3.2%). For White men, the following nations/geographic entities have 10 or more honorees: Canada, 16 (3.9% of the total 408 honorees); Germany, 14 (3.4%); and Israel and Iran each, 10 (2.5%). For White women, the following nations/geographic entities have 4 or more honorees: Cuba and Iran each, 8 (2% of the total 408 honorees); Mexico, 7 (1.7%); Germany, 6 (1.5%); and Australia, England, UK, and Russia each, 4 (1%). For Asians, the following nations/geographic entities have 5 or more honorees: India, 28 (6.9% of the total 408 honorees); China, 27 (6.6%); South Korea, Taiwan and Vietnam each, 7 (1.7%); the Philippines, 6 (1.5%); and Japan and Pakistan each, 5 (1.2%). For Asian men, the following nations/geographic entities have 4 or more honorees: India, 23 (5.6% of the total 408 honorees); China, 20 (4.9%); South Korea, 6 (1.5%); Taiwan, 5 (1.2%); and Vietnam, 4 (1%). For Asian women, the following nations/geographic entities have 3 or more honorees: China, 7 (1.7% of the total 408 honorees); India, 5 (1.2%); and Japan, Pakistan, the Philippines, and Vietnam each 3 (0.7%). For Blacks, the following nations/geographic entities have 2 or more honorees: the Dominican Republic, 5 (1.2% of the total 408 honorees); Haiti, 4 (1%); Jamaica and Nigeria each, 3 (0.7%); and Ethiopia, Ghana, and Saint Vincent and the Grenadines each, 2 (0.5%). For Black men, the following nations/geographic entities have 2 or more honorees: the Dominican Republic, 5 (1.2%); Haiti and Nigeria each, 3 (0.7%); Ethiopia, Ghana, Jamaica, and Saint Vincent and the Grenadines each, 2 (0.5%). Of the 4 Black women, 1 (0.25%) each is from: Antigua and Barbuda, Haiti, Jamaica, and Somalia. Finally, the only American Indian is from Bolivia (Table 5).

Table 5. Previous Nationality/Citizenship of Carnegie Corporation of New York's "Pride of America" Honorees, by Race and Sex, 2006-2015
N=408 honorees, from 87 nations/geographic entities

All Country	#	%	Men	%	Women	%	White	%	Men	%	Women	%	Asian	%	Men	%	Women	%	Black	%	Men	%	Women	%
Afghanistan	3	0.7	3	1.0			3	1.1	3	1.6		0.0		0.0		0.0		0.0		0.0		0.0		0.0
Algeria	1	0.2	1	0.3			1	0.4	1	0.5		0.0		0.0		0.0		0.0		0.0		0.0		0.0
Antigua and Barbuda	1	0.2			1	0.8				0.0		0.0		0.0		0.0		0.0	1	2.9		0.0	1	25.0
Argentina	4	1.0	4	1.4			4	1.5	4	2.1		0.0		0.0		0.0		0.0		0.0		0.0		0.0
Armenia	1	0.2	1	0.3			1	0.4	1	0.5		0.0		0.0		0.0		0.0		0.0		0.0		0.0
Australia	8	2.0	4	1.4	4	3.4	8	3.0	4	2.1	4	4.8		0.0		0.0		0.0		0.0		0.0		0.0
Austria	8	2.0	7	2.4	1	0.8	8	3.0	7	3.7	1	1.2		0.0		0.0		0.0		0.0		0.0		0.0
Azerbaijan	1	0.2	1	0.3			1	0.4	1	0.5		0.0		0.0		0.0		0.0		0.0		0.0		0.0
Bangladesh	1	0.2	1	0.3				0.0		0.0		0.0	1	1.0	1	1.4		0.0		0.0		0.0		0.0
Belarus	1	0.2			1	0.8	1	0.4		0.0	1	1.2		0.0		0.0		0.0		0.0		0.0		0.0
Benin	1	0.2	1	0.3				0.0		0.0		0.0		0.0		0.0		0.0	1	2.9	1	3.3		0.0
Bolivia	2	0.5	1	0.3	1	0.8	1	0.4		0.0	1	1.2		0.0		0.0		0.0		0.0		0.0		0.0
Bulgaria	2	0.5	2	0.7			2	0.7	2	1.1		0.0		0.0		0.0		0.0		0.0		0.0		0.0
Canada	20	4.9	16	5.5	4	3.4	19	7.0	16	8.6	3	3.6	1	1.0		0.0	1	3.2		0.0		0.0		0.0
Cote d'Ivoire	1	0.2	1	0.3				0.0		0.0		0.0		0.0		0.0		0.0	1	2.9	1	3.3		0.0
China	28	6.9	21	7.3	7	5.9	1	0.4	1	0.5		0.0	27	26.5	20	28.2	7	22.6		0.0		0.0		0.0
Colombia	2	0.5	1	0.3	1	0.8	2	0.7	1	0.5	1	1.2		0.0		0.0		0.0		0.0		0.0		0.0
Costa Rica	1	0.2	1	0.3			1	0.4	1	0.5		0.0		0.0		0.0		0.0		0.0		0.0		0.0
Croatia	1	0.2			1	0.8	1	0.4		0.0	1	1.2		0.0		0.0		0.0		0.0		0.0		0.0
Cuba	17	4.2	9	3.1	8	6.7	17	6.3	9	4.8	8	9.5		0.0		0.0		0.0		0.0		0.0		0.0
Cyprus	1	0.2	1	0.3			1	0.4	1	0.5		0.0		0.0		0.0		0.0		0.0		0.0		0.0
Czech Republic	6	1.5	3	1.0	3	2.5	6	2.2	3	1.6	3	3.6		0.0		0.0		0.0		0.0		0.0		0.0
Democratic Republic of Congo	1	0.2	1	0.3				0.0		0.0		0.0		0.0		0.0		0.0	1	2.9	1	3.3		0.0
Dominican Republic	7	1.7	6	2.1	1	0.8	2	0.7	1	0.5	1	1.2		0.0		0.0		0.0	5	14.7	5	16.7		0.0
Egypt	6	1.5	5	1.7	1	0.8	6	2.2	5	2.7	1	1.2		0.0		0.0		0.0		0.0		0.0		0.0
England, UK	22	5.4	17	5.9	5	4.2	19	7.0	15	8.0	4	4.8	2	2.0	1	1.4	1	3.2	1	2.9	1	3.3		0.0

Table 5 continues...

All Country	#	%	Men	%	Women	%	White	%	Men	%	Women	%	Asian	%	Men	%	Women	%	Black	%	Men	%	Women	%
Eritrea	1	0.2	1	0.3			0.0		0.0		0.0		0.0		0.0		0.0		1	2.9	1	3.3	0.0
Estonia	1	0.2	1	0.3			1	0.4	1	0.5	0.0		0.0		0.0		0.0		0.0		0.0		0.0
Ethiopia	2	0.5	2	0.7			0.0		0.0		0.0		0.0		0.0		0.0		2	5.9	2	6.7	0.0
France	5	1.2	4	1.4	1	0.8	4	1.5	3	1.6	1	1.2	1	1.0	1	1.4	0.0		0.0		0.0		0.0
Germany	20	4.9	14	4.8	6	5.0	20	7.4	14	7.5	6	7.1	0.0		0.0		0.0		0.0		0.0		0.0
Ghana	2	0.5	2	0.7			0.0		0.0		0.0		0.0		0.0		0.0		2	5.9	2	6.7	0.0
Greece	3	0.7	2	0.7	1	0.8	3	1.1	2	1.1	1	1.2	0.0		0.0		0.0		0.0		0.0		0.0
Guyana	1	0.2	1	0.3			0.0		0.0		0.0		0.0		0.0		0.0		1	2.9	1	3.3	0.0
Haiti	4	1.0	3	1.0	1	0.8	0.0		0.0		0.0		0.0		0.0		0.0		4	11.8	3	10.0	1	25.0
Hong Kong, China	1	0.2	1	0.3			0.0		0.0		0.0		1	1.0	1	1.4	0.0		0.0		0.0		0.0
Hungary	6	1.5	5	1.7	1	0.8	6	2.2	5	2.7	1	1.2	0.0		0.0		0.0		0.0		0.0		0.0
India	29	7.1	24	8.3	5	4.2	1	0.4	1	0.5	0.0		28	27.5	23	32.4	5	16.1	0.0		0.0		0.0
Indonesia	1	0.2		0.0	1	0.8	1	0.4		0.0	1	1.2	0.0		0.0		0.0		0.0		0.0		0.0
Iran	18	4.4	10	3.5	8	6.7	18	6.6	10	5.3	8	9.5	0.0		0.0		0.0		0.0		0.0		0.0
Ireland	6	1.5	4	1.4	2	1.7	6	2.2	4	2.1	2	2.4	0.0		0.0		0.0		0.0		0.0		0.0
Israel	13	3.2	10	3.5	3	2.5	13	4.8	10	5.3	3	3.6	0.0		0.0		0.0		0.0		0.0		0.0
Italy	6	1.5	4	1.4	2	1.7	6	2.2	4	2.1	2	2.4	0.0		0.0		0.0		0.0		0.0		0.0
Jamaica	3	0.7	2	0.7	1	0.8	0.0		0.0		0.0		0.0		0.0		0.0		3	8.8	2	6.7	1	25.0
Japan	5	1.2	2	0.7	3	2.5	0.0		0.0		0.0		5	4.9	2	2.8	3	9.7	0.0		0.0		0.0
Kenya	1	0.2	1	0.3			0.0		0.0		0.0		0.0		0.0		0.0		1	2.9	1	3.3	0.0
Kosovo	1	0.2	1	0.3			1	0.4	1	0.5	0.0		0.0		0.0		0.0		0.0		0.0		0.0
Laos	2	0.5			2	1.7	0.0		0.0		0.0		2	2.0	0.0		2	6.5	0.0		0.0		0.0
Latvia	2	0.5	1	0.3	1	0.8	2	0.7	1	0.5	1	1.2	0.0		0.0		0.0		0.0		0.0		0.0
Lebanon	5	1.2	4	1.4	1	0.8	5	1.8	4	2.1	1	1.2	0.0		0.0		0.0		0.0		0.0		0.0
Lithuania	1	0.2	1	0.3			1	0.4	1	0.5	0.0		0.0		0.0		0.0		0.0		0.0		0.0
Mexico	14	3.4	7	2.4	7	5.9	14	5.2	7	3.7	7	8.3	0.0		0.0		0.0		0.0		0.0		0.0
Morocco	1	0.2	1	0.3			1	0.4	1	0.5	0.0		0.0		0.0		0.0		0.0		0.0		0.0
Mozambique	1	0.2		0.0	1	0.8	1	0.4		0.0	1	1.2	0.0		0.0		0.0		0.0		0.0		0.0
Netherlands	2	0.5	2	0.7			2	0.7	2	1.1	0.0		0.0		0.0		0.0		0.0		0.0		0.0
New Zealand	1	0.2	1	0.3			1	0.4	1	0.5	0.0		0.0		0.0		0.0		0.0		0.0		0.0

Table 5 continues…

All Country	#	%	Men	%	Women	%	White	%	Men	%	Women	%	Asian	%	Men	%	Women	%	Black	%	Men	%	Women	%
Nigeria	3	0.7	3	1.0		0.0		0.0		0.0		0.0		0.0		0.0	3	8.8	3	10.0		0.0
Norway	2	0.5	2	0.7		2	0.7	2	1.1		0.0		0.0		0.0		0.0		0.0		0.0		0.0
Pakistan	5	1.2	2	0.7	3	2.5		0.0		0.0		0.0	5	4.9	2	2.8	3	9.7		0.0		0.0		0.0
Peru	3	0.7	2	0.7	1	0.8	3	1.1	2	1.1	1	1.2		0.0		0.0		0.0		0.0		0.0		0.0
Philippines	7	1.7	3	1.0	4	3.4	1	0.4		0.0	1	1.2	6	5.9	3	4.2	3	9.7		0.0		0.0		0.0
Poland	5	1.2	2	0.7	3	2.5	5	1.8	2	1.1	3	3.6		0.0		0.0		0.0		0.0		0.0		0.0
Romania	3	0.7	2	0.7	1	0.8	3	1.1	2	1.1	1	1.2		0.0		0.0		0.0		0.0		0.0		0.0
Russia	13	3.2	9	3.1	4	3.4	13	4.8	9	4.8	4	4.8		0.0		0.0		0.0		0.0		0.0		0.0
Saint Vincent and the Grenadines	2	0.5	2	0.7		0.0		0.0		0.0		0.0		0.0		0.0	2	5.9	2	6.7		0.0
Scotland, UK	3	0.7	2	0.7	1	0.8	3	1.1	2	1.1	1	1.2		0.0		0.0		0.0		0.0		0.0		0.0
Serbia	2	0.5	1	0.3	1	0.8	2	0.7	1	0.5	1	1.2		0.0		0.0		0.0		0.0		0.0		0.0
Sierra Leone	1	0.2	1	0.3		0.0		0.0		0.0		0.0		0.0		0.0	1	2.9	1	3.3		0.0
Slovakia	1	0.2	1	0.3		1	0.4	1	0.5		0.0		0.0		0.0		0.0		0.0		0.0		0.0
Slovenia	1	0.2	1	0.3		1	0.4	1	0.5		0.0		0.0		0.0		0.0		0.0		0.0		0.0
Somalia	1	0.2		1	0.8		0.0		0.0		0.0		0.0		0.0		0.0	1	2.9	0.0	1	25.0
South Africa	6	1.5	4	1.4	2	1.7	5	1.8	3	1.6	2	2.4	1	1.0	1	1.4		0.0		0.0		0.0
South Korea	7	1.7	6	2.1	1	0.8		0.0		0.0		0.0	7	6.9	6	8.5	1	3.2		0.0		0.0		0.0
South Sudan	1	0.2	1	0.3		0.0		0.0		0.0		0.0		0.0		0.0	1	2.9	1	3.3		0.0
Spain	5	1.2	5	1.7		5	1.8	5	2.7		0.0		0.0		0.0		0.0		0.0		0.0
Sweden	3	0.7	1	0.3	2	1.7	3	1.1	1	0.5	2	2.4		0.0		0.0		0.0		0.0		0.0		0.0
Switzerland	1	0.2		0.0	1	0.8	1	0.4		0.0	1	1.2		0.0		0.0		0.0		0.0		0.0
Syria	2	0.5	2	0.7		2	0.7	2	1.1		0.0		0.0		0.0		0.0		0.0		0.0
Taiwan	7	1.7	5	1.7	2	1.7		0.0		0.0		0.0	7	6.9	5	7.0	2	6.5		0.0		0.0		0.0
Thailand	1	0.2	1	0.3		0.0		0.0		0.0	1	1.0	1	1.4		0.0		0.0		0.0
Turkey	1	0.2	1	0.3		1	0.4	1	0.5		0.0		0.0		0.0		0.0		0.0		0.0		0.0
Ukraine	3	0.7	2	0.7	1	0.8	3	1.1	2	1.1	1	1.2		0.0		0.0		0.0		0.0		0.0		0.0
Uzbekistan	1	0.2	1	0.3		1	0.4	1	0.5		0.0		0.0		0.0		0.0		0.0		0.0		0.0

Table 5 continues…

All Country	#	%	Men	%	Women	%	White	%	Men	%	Women	%	Asian	%	Men	%	Women	%	Black	%	Men	%	Women	%
Venezuela	4	1.0	3	1.0	1	0.8	3	1.1	2	1.1	1	1.2		0.0		0.0		0.0	1	2.9	1	3.3		0
Vietnam	7	1.7	4	1.4	3	2.5		0.0		0.0		0.0	7	6.9	4	5.6	3	9.7		0.0		0.0		0
Zambia	1	0.2		0.0	1	0.8	1	0.4		0.0	1	1.2		0.0		0.0		0.0		0.0		0.0		0
Zimbabwe	1	0.2	1	0.3				0.0		0.0		0.0		0.0		0.0		0.0	1	2.9	1	3.3		0
Total	408	100.0	289	100.0	119	100.0	271	100.0	187	100.0	84	100.0	102	100.0	71	100.0	31	100.0	34	100.0	30	100.0	4	10

Source: Compiled and computed from June 24, 2015, to January 6, 2016, based on data from: "Great Immigrants: The Pride of America". Carnegie Corporation of New York. http://greatimmigrants.carnegie.org/pride-america/.

Geographic Region of Previous Country of Citizenship of Carnegie Corporation of New York's "Pride of America" Honorees, by Race and Sex, 2006-2015

As the data in the concept section above show, examining the costs and benefits of the brain drain is not limited to countries alone, but to entire regions or continents. When a Nigerian doctor relocates to the United States, all of West Africa or even Africa itself feels the impact. Just as the United States and Canada, or even Mexico, benefits from this individual's skills, due to the movement of people among these three latter countries because of the 1994 North American Free Trade Agreement (NAFTA). Research studies on competition among countries have utilized world geographic regions as a variable (Kaba, 2013, 2012b; Lyytinen et al., 2007). In his examination of the *Times Higher Education*-QS top 200 universities in the world in 2009, Kaba (2012) finds that 85 (42.5%) were located in Europe; 66 (33%) in the Americas; 36 (18%) in Asia; 12 (6%) in Oceania; and 1 (0.5%) in Africa (p.10).

Table 6 presents a regional or continental breakdown of the countries of previous nationality or citizenship of all 408 "Pride of America" honorees. According to Table 6, 147 (36%) honorees are from Asia (104 men and 43 women), 135 (33.1%) from Europe (96 men and 39 women), 85 (20.8%) from the Americas (58 men and 27 women), 32 (7.8%) from Africa (26 men and 6 women), and 9 (2.2%) from Oceania (5 men and 4 women). Among the various racial groups, 131 (32.1% of the total 408 honorees) Whites are from Europe (93 men and 38 women), 66 (16.2%) from the Americas (43 men and 23 women), 50 (12.5%) from Asia (36 men and 14 women), 15 (3.7%) from Africa (10 men and 5 women), and 9 (2.2%) from Oceana (5 men and 4 women). For Asians, 97 (23.8% of the total 408 honorees) of them are from Asia (68 men and 29 women), 3 (0.7%) from Europe (2 men and 1 women), and 1 (0.25%) each from Africa (man) and the Americas (woman). For Blacks, 17 (4.2% of the total 408 honorees) are from the Americas (14 men and 3 women), 16 (3.9%) from Africa (15 men and 1 women), and 1 (0.25%) man from Europe. Finally, there is 1 (0.25%) American Indian man from the Americas (Table 6).

Table 6. Geographic Region of Previous Country of Citizenship of Carnegie Corporation of New York's "Pride of America" Honorees, by Race and Sex, 2006-2015
N=408

Region	All #	%	Men	%	Women	%	White	%	Men	%	Women	%	Asian	%	Men	%	Women	%	Black	%	Men	%	Women	%	AI	%	Men	%
Eastern Africa	9	28.1	6	23.1	3	50.0	2	13.3			2	40							7	43.8	6	40.0	1	100				
Middle Africa	1	3.1	1	3.8															1	6.3	1	6.7						
Northern Africa	8	25.0	7	26.9	1	16.7	8	53.3	7	70.0	1	20																
Southern Africa	6	18.8	4	15.4	2	33.3	5	33.3	3	30.0	2	40	1	100	1	100												
Western Africa	8	25.0	8	30.8							0								8	50.0	8	53.3						
Africa	32	100.0	26	100.0	6	100.0	15	100.0	10	100.0	5	100	1	100	1	100			16	100	15	100	1	100				
% Within Group								100		66.6		33.3				100				100		93.8		6.3				
% of Africa			81.3		18.7		42.9		31.3		15.6		3.1		3.1				50		46.8		3.1					
% of Overall Total		7.8		9		5		5.5		5.4		6		1		1.4				47		50		25				
Northern America	20		16	80	4	20	19		16	84.2	3	15.8	1		1	100												
% of Americas		23.5		27.6		14.8		28.8		37.2		13		100				100										
% of Overall Total		4.9		5.5		3.4		7		8.6		3.6		0.99				3.2										
Central America	15	23.1	8	19.0	7	30.4	15	31.9	8	29.6	7	35								0.0		0.0	0					
South America	16	24.6	12	28.6	4	17.4	13	27.7	9	33.3	4	20							2	11.8	2	14.3	0		1	100	1	1
Caribbean	34	52.3	22	52.4	12	52.2	19	40.4	10	37.0	9	45							15	88.2	12	85.7	3	100				
Latin America & Caribbean	65	100.0	42	100.0	23	100.0	47	100.0	27	100.0	20	100							17	100	14	100	3	100	1	100	1	1
% within Region			64.6		35.4		72.3		41.5		30.8								26		21.5		4.6		1.5		1	
% of Americas		76.5		72.4		85.2		71.2		62.8		87								100		100		100		100		1	
% of Overall Total		15.9		14.6		5.9		5.5		4.3		8.3																	
Americas	85		58	68.2	27	31.8	66		43	65.2	23	34.9	1				1		17		14	82.4	3	18	1		1	
% of Overall Total		20.8		20.1		22.7		24.4		23		27.4		0.99				3.2		50		46.7		75		100		1
Central Asia	2	1.4	2	1.9			2	4	2	5.6																		

Table 6 continues…

Region	All #	%	Men	%	Women	%	White	%	Men	%	Women	%	Asian	%	Men	%	Women	%	Black	%	Men	%	Women	%	AI	%	Men	%
Eastern Asia	48	32.7	35	33.7	13	30.2	1	2	1	2.8			47	48.5	34	50.0	13	44.8										
Southern Asia	56	38.1	40	38.5	16	37.2	22	44	14	38.9	8	57.1	34	35.1	26	38.2	8	27.6										
Southeastern Asia	18	12.2	8	7.7	10	23.3	2	4			2	14.3	16	16.5	8	11.8	8	27.6										
Western Asia	23	15.6	19	18.3	4	9.3	23	46	19	52.8	4	28.6																
Asia	147	100.0	104	100.0	43	100.0	50	100	36	100.0	14	100.0	97	100.0	68	100.0	29	100										
% within Group									100		72		28				70.1		29.1									
% of Asia			70.7		29.3		34		24.5		9.5		66		46.3		19.7											
% of Overall Total		36		36		36.1		18.5		19.2		16.7		95.1		95.8		93.5										
Eastern Europe	40	29.6	26	27.1	14	35.9	40	30.5	26	28.0	14	36.8																
Northern Europe	40	29.6	29	30.2	11	28.2	37	28.2	27	29.0	10	26.3	2	66.7	1	50.0	1	50.0	1	50.0	1	50.0						
Southern Europe	19	14.1	14	14.6	5	12.8	19	14.5	14	15.1	5	13.2	0.0															
Western Europe	36	26.7	27	28.1	9	23.1	35	26.7	26	28.0	9	23.7	1	33.3	1	50.0		50.0		50.0		50.0						
Europe	135	100.0	96	100.0	39	100.0	131	100.0	93	100.0	38	100.0	3	100.0	2	100	1	100	1	100	1	100						
% Within Group									71		29				66.6		33.3				100							
% of Europe			71		29		97		72		28		2.2		1.5		0.7		0.7		0.7							
% of Overall Total		33.1		33.2		32.8		48.3		49.7		45.2		2.9		2.8		3.2		2.9		3.3						
Oceania	9		5		4		9		5		4																
% of Overall Total		2.2		1.7		3.4		3.3		2.7		4.8																
Overall Total	408		289		119		271		187		84		102		71		31		34		30		4		1		1	

Source: Compiled and computed from June 24, 2015, to January 6, 2016, based on data from: "Great Immigrants: The Pride of America". Carnegie Corporation of New York. http://greatimmigrants.carnegie.org/pride-america/; The United Nations classifications of regions can be found at: "Composition of macro geographical (continental) regions, geographical sub-regions, and selected economic and other groupings," United Nations Statistics Division, Department of Economic and Social Affairs. Retrieved on May 19, 2016: http://unstats.un.org/unsd/methods/m49/m49regin.htm.

List of Previous Nationality/Country, their U.S. Population, Country's Population, GDP, and GDP Per Capita of Carnegie Corporation of New York's "Pride of America" Honorees, 2006-2015

Table 7 presents the countries/nations or geographic entities of previous citizenships of the "Pride of America" honorees, their ancestry population in the United States, the 2015 population of their countries of previous citizenship, the Gross Domestic Product (GDP), and GDP per capita of those nations. The U.S. populations of these various nationalities or ancestries are as of 2014. However, as the 2014 data were not available for a number of them, this author decided to present data for any available years for those nations.

According to Table 7, the countries or ancestries with 10 million or more in the United States in 2014 or before are Germany, 46.1 million; Ireland, 33.2 million; Mexico, 31.8 million (2010); England, 24.4 million; and Italy, 17.2 million. The nations listed in Table 7 have both the largest and smallest populations in the world. For example, 11 of the top 13 most populous nations (excluding the United States), with at least, 100 million people and some of the smallest nations as of 2015 are listed in Table 7. China (1.37 billion people), India (1.25 billion people), Indonesia (256 million people, fourth after the United States), Pakistan (199 million people, after Brazil, with over 204 million people), Nigeria (182 million people), Bangladesh (169 million people), Russia (142 million people), Japan (127 million people), Mexico (122 million people), the Philippines (101 million people), and Ethiopia (100 million people). Saint Vincent and the Grenadines (102,627 people) and Antigua and Barbuda (92,436 people) are among small nations with honorees represented in this study.

Table 7 also shows that many of the countries listed here have both the world's highest and lowest GDP and GDP per capita. For example, 18 nations with a 2014 GDP of $1 trillion or more, are listed in Table 7. China ($18.090 trillion), India ($7.411 trillion), Japan ($4.767 trillion), Germany ($3.748 trillion), Russia ($3.577 trillion), Indonesia ($2.686 trillion), France ($2.591 trillion), the United Kingdom (which includes England, Scotland, Wales, and Northern Ireland) ($2.569 trillion), Mexico ($2.149 trillion), South Korea ($1.784 trillion), Canada ($1.596 trillion), Spain ($$1.572 trillion), Turkey ($1.515 trillion), Iran ($1.357 trillion), Australia ($1.1 trillion), Taiwan ($1.079 trillion), Thailand

($1.070 trillion), and Nigeria ($1.053 trillion). There are 13 nations with GDP per capita of almost $40,000 or higher in 2014 listed in Table 7: Norway ($67,200), Switzerland ($58,100), Hong Kong, China ($55,100), Ireland ($51,300), the Netherlands ($48,000), Austria ($47,100), Australia ($46,600), Germany and Sweden each ($46,200), Taiwan ($46,000), Canada ($45,000), France ($40,500), and the United Kingdom ($39,800). The following nations had the world's lowest GDP per capita in 2014 (under $2,200): Somalia ($600); the Democratic Republic of Congo ($700); Eritrea and Mozambique each ($1,200); Ethiopia ($1,600); Haiti ($1,800); Afghanistan and Benin each ($1,900); and Sierra Leone, South Sudan, and Zimbabwe each ($2,100).

The data in Table 7 reveal that the brain drain phenomenon affects all nations alike, whether they are large and small or rich and poor nations. There were less than 98,000 people of Afghan descent, but they have 3 honorees, whereas Argentina has 4 honorees, but had 224,952 ancestral members in 2010. Cuba has 1.8 million country of origin members in 2010, but 17 honorees, whereas England had 24.4 million ancestral members, but 22 honorees. There were 148,514 people with Israeli descent listed, but Israel has 13 honorees, whereas Russia has 2.8 million country of origin members, but has 13 honorees. Ireland had almost 33.2 million ancestral members, but has only 6 honorees, whereas India and China had 3.2 million and 3.8 million ancestral members, respectively, but 29 and 28 honorees, respectively. Taiwan has 215,441 ancestral members, but 7 honorees, whereas Italy has 17.2 million ancestral members, but 6 honorees (Table 7).

One explanation for this can be found in the total populations of the ancestry nations or countries, whereby a large country such as India or China has the potential to have many talented people. Another reason might be that for poor countries, the United States is one nation where their honorees could have the opportunity to hone their talents or skills and be recognized for those skills.

Table 7. List of Previous Nationality/Country, their U.S. Ancestry Population, Country's Population, GDP, and GDP Per Capita of Carnegie Corporation of New York's "Pride of America" Honorees, 2006-2015

N=408 honorees, from 87 nations/geographic entities

Country	# of Honorees	Ancestry Population in U.S. (2014)	Population (2015 est.)	GDP (2014 est.)	GDP Per Capita
Afghanistan	3	97,865	32,564,342	60.81	1,900
Algeria	1	10,880*	39,542,166	548.6	13,900
Antigua and Barbuda	1	18 325*	92,436	2.032	23,000
Argentina	4	224,952**	43,431,886	951	22,300
Armenia	1	461,076	3,056,382	24.37	8,200
Australia	8	98,397	22,751,014	1,100	46,600
Austria	8	702,772	8,665,550	396.8	47,100
Azerbaijan	1	14 205*	9,780,780	165.9	17,800
Bangladesh	1	147,300***	168,957,745	536.5	3,400
Belarus	1	38 505*	9,589,689	172.8	18,200
Benin	1	1,125*	10,448,647	19.86	1,900
Bolivia	2	99,210**	10,800,882	70.28	6,200
Bulgaria	2	90,981	7,186,893	129.1	17,900
Canada	20	678,113	35,099,836	1,596	45,000
China	28	3,779,732***	1,367,485,388	18,090	13,200
Colombia	2	908,734**	46,736,728	642.5	13,500
Costa Rica	1	126,418**	4,814,144	71.23	14,900
Cote d'Ivoire	1	7 175*	23,295,302	71.67	3,100
Croatia	1	419,647	4,464,844	88.73	20,900
Cuba	17	1,785,547**	11,031,433	128.5	10,200
Cyprus	1	6,752	1,189,197	27.52	30,900
Czech Republic	6	1,419,630	10,644,842	315.9	30,000

Table 7 continues...

Country	# of Honorees	Ancestry Population in U.S. (2014)	Population (2015 est.)	GDP (2014 est.)	GDP Per Capita
Democratic Republic of Congo	1	4 990*	79,375,136	57.78	700
Dominican Republic	7	1,414,703**	10,478,756	138.5	14,000
Egypt	6	239,010	88,487,396	946.6	10,900
England, UK	22	24,382,182	54,316,600*****	2,569*****	39,800*****
Eritrea	1	17 520 *	6,527,689	7.842	1,200
Estonia	1	29,453	1,265,420	36.78	27,900
Ethiopia	2	259,744	99,465,819	145.1	1,600
France	5	8,153,515	66,553,766	2,591	40,500
Germany	20	46,047,113	80,854,408	3,748	46,200
Ghana	2	117,247	26,327,649	108.5	4,100
Greece	3	1,295,703	10,775,643	285.3	26,000
Guyana	1	234,591	735,222	5.534	6,900
Haiti	4	984,514	10,110,019	18.38	1,800
Hong Kong, China	1	..	7,141,106	400.4	55,100
Hungary	6	1,406,350	9,897,541	247.1	25,000
India	29	3,183,063***	1,251,695,584	7,411	5,800
Indonesia	1	95,270***	255,993,674	2,686	10,700
Iran	18	452,815	81,824,270	1,357	17,400
Ireland	6	33,147,639	4,892,305	236.4	51,300
Israel	13	148,514	8,049,314	272.1	33,100
Italy	6	17,220,604	61,855,120	2.135	35,100
Jamaica	3	1,087,185	2,950,210	24.1	8,600
Japan	5	1,304,286***	126,919,659	4,767	37,500
Kenya	1	62,810	45,925,301	133	3,100
Kosovo	1	..	1,870,981	16.92	..

Table 7 continues...

Country	# of Honorees	Ancestry Population in U.S. (2014)	Population (2015 est.)	GDP (2014 est.)	GDP Per Capita
Laos	2	232,130***	6,911,544	34.53	5,000
Latvia	2	87,817	1,986,705	48.36	23,800
Lebanon	5	506,470	6,184,701	81.42	18,100
Lithuania	1	652,790	2,884,433	79.93	27,300
Mexico	14	31,798,258**	121,736,809	2,149	18,000
Morocco	1	101,211	33,322,699	259.2	7,800
Mozambique	1	2 025*	25,303,113	31.21	1,200
Netherlands	2	4,243,067	16,947,904	808.8	48,000
New Zealand	1	18,638	4,438,393	160.8	35,300
Nigeria	3	322,231	181,562,056	1,053	6,100
Norway	2	4,444,566	5,207,689	346.3	67,200
Pakistan	5	409,163***	199,085,847	884.2	4,700
Peru	3	531,358**	30,444,999	372.7	11,900
Philippines	7	3,416,840***	100,998,376	693.4	7,000
Poland	5	9,249,392	38,562,189	959.8	25,200
Romania	3	459,810	21,666,350	393.8	19,700
Russia	13	2,762,830	142,423,773	3,577	24,400
Saint Vincent and the Grenadines	2	..	102,627	1.174	10,700
Scotland, UK	3	5,365,154	5,347,600*****	..	..
Serbia	2	181,171	7,176,794	95.84	13,400
Sierra Leone	1	21,737	5,879,098	12.8	2,100
Slovakia	1	706,662	5,445,027	153.2	28,300
Slovenia	1	178,273	1,983,412	61.56	29,900
Somalia	1	151,838	10,616,380	5.896	600
South Africa	6	60,037	53,675,563	707.1	13,100
South Korea	7	1,706,822***	49,115,196	1,784	35,400
South Sudan	1	..	12,042,910	23.5	2,100

Table 7 continues...

Country	# of Honorees	Ancestry Population in U.S. (2014)	Population (2015 est.)	GDP (2014 est.)	GDP Per Capita
Spain	5	635,253**	48,146,134	1,572	33,800
Sweden	3	4 000 000****	9,801,616	450.5	46,200
Switzerland	1	..	8,121,830	473.3	58,100
Syria	2	170,066	17,064,854	107.6	5,100
Taiwan	7	215,441***	23,415,126	1,079	46,000
Thailand	1	237,583***	67,976,405	1,070	15,600
Turkey	1	206,911	79,414,269	1,515	19,700
Ukraine	3	984,157	44,429,471	371.8	8,700
Uzbekistan	1	23 030*	29,199,942	172.3	5,600
Venezuela	4	215,023**	29,275,460	540.9	17,800
Vietnam	7	1,737,433***	94,348,835	512.6	5,700
Zambia	1	5 985 *	15,066,266	61.39	4,100
Zimbabwe	1	7,642	14,229,541	27.26	2,100

Source: "People Reporting Ancestry," 2016.
Note:

-*The ancestry data are from the United States Census Bureau for the year 2000 for the following nations. The source is cited for each ancestry group by the U.S. Census as follows. "Table FBP-1. Profile of Selected Demographic and Social Characteristics: 2000 Population Universe: People Born in [name of group here],"
Algeria: https://www.census.gov/population/foreign/files/stp 159/STP-159 algeria.pdf; **Azerbaijan**:http://www.census.gov/population/cen2000/stp-159/STP 159 Azerbaijan.pdf; **Benin**: http://www.census.gov/population/cen2000/stp-159/STP-159-benin.pdf; **Antigua and Barbuda**; http://www.census.gov/population/cen2000/stp 159/stp159 antigua_and_barbuda.pdf; **Belarus**: http://www.census.gov/population/cen2000/stp-159/STP-159 Belarus.pdf; **Ivory Coast**: https://www.census.gov/population/foreign/files/stp 159/STP 159 ivory_coast.pdf; **Democratic Republic**

of Congo: http://www.census.gov/population/cen2000/stp 159/STP 159-democratic_republic_congo.pdf; **Eritrea**:http://www.census.gov/population/cen2000/stp 159/STP 159 eritrea.pdf; **Mozambique**: http://www.census.gov/population/cen2000/stp-159/STP 159 mozambique.pdf; **Zambia**: https://www.census.gov/population/foreign/files/stp-159/STP 159 zambia.pdf; and **Uzbekistan**: https://www.census.gov/population/foreign/files/stp-159/STP-159-uzbekistan.pdf.

-**The ancestry data for the following groups are as of 2010: Argentina, Bolivia, Colombia, Costa Rica, Cuba, Dominican Republic, Mexico, Peru, Spain and Venezuela (Source: Ennis, Sharon R., Ríos-Vargas, Merarys., and Albert, Nora G. 2011, May. "The Hispanic Population: 2010," U.S. Census Bureau. Retrieved on May 18 2016 from: http://www.census.gov/prod/cen2010/briefs/c2010br-04.pdf) (p.3).

-***The ancestry data for the following groups are as of 2010: Bangladesh, China, India, Indonesia, Japan, Laos, Pakistan, Philippines, South Korea, Taiwan, Thailand and Vietnam (Source: Hoeffel, Elizabeth M., Rastogi, Sonya., Kim, Myoung Ouk., and Shahid, Hasan. 2012, March. "The Asian Population: 2010," United States Census Bureau. Retrieved on May 18 2016 from: https://www.census.gov/prod/cen2010/briefs/c2010br 11.pdf?cssp=SERP (pp.14-15).

-****The ancestry data for Sweden is for the year 2000 and can be found at: Suchan et al. (2007, p.139).

-*****The country population for England and Scotland are as of 2014: "Statistical bulletin: Annual   Mid-year Population Estimates: 2014," 2015, June 25. Estimates of the usual resident population in the United Kingdom and its constituent countries. Office of National Statistics. Retrieved on December 28, 2015 from:
http://www.ons.gov.uk/ons/rel/pop-estimate/population-estimates-for-uk--england-and-wales--scotland-and-northern-ireland/mid-2014/mid-year-population-estimates-for-the-uk-2014.html (p.1); The GDP and GDP per capita for England, UK is for the entire United Kingdom.

Educational Attainment (Highest/Terminal Higher Education Degree Earned) of "Pride of America" Honorees, 2006-2015

In the United States, one's level of education (academic degree or diploma) is associated or correlated with income. For the most part, the higher one's level of education, the higher their annual income (Allen, 2006; Bideshi & Kposowa, 2012; Guo, 2015; Hunt, 2011; Kaba, 2005; Kaushal, 2011; Li & Skop, 2010, p.300; Painter II, 2015; Peri & Sparber, 2011; Wai, 2015; Wai & Rindermann, 2015). According to Kaba (2005) during his/her working life, an adult with a high school diploma is expected, "… on average, to earn $1.2 million; those with a bachelor's degree, $2.1 million; and people with a master's degree, $2.5 million…. People with doctoral [degrees,] ($3.4 million) and professional degrees ($4.4 million) do even better" (p.14).

The United States leads all nations in the enrollment of international students in its colleges and universities. For example, in the 2014-2015 academic year, there were 974,926 international students enrolled in U.S. colleges and universities: undergraduates, 398,824 (41%); graduates, 362,228 (37.2%); non-degree students, 93,587 (9.6%); and optional practical training students, 120,287 (12.3%). The top five sending countries were China (31.2%), India (13.6%), South Korea (6.5%), Saudi Arabia (6.1%), and Canada (2.8%) ("International Students in the U.S.: 2015 "Fast Facts,'" 2016). International students have a big impact in U.S. graduate schools, especially in doctoral programs. For example, in 2014, of the 54,070 doctorate degrees awarded to students in the United States, U.S. citizens and permanent residents accounted for 34,005 (62.9%), and temporary visa holders accounted for 15,852 (29.3%) ("TABLE 17. Doctorate recipients, by citizenship status," 2016; also see Han et al., 2015, pp.7-8). The figure for non-U.S. citizens is higher if one extracts permanent residents from the 34,005 students.

Through extensive research, this author decided to provide any available data on the level and types of terminal or highest higher education degrees earned by the "Pride of America" honorees. Table 8 presents such data: 323 (79.2% of the total 408 honorees) honorees earned 352 highest or terminal degrees combined, from associate degrees to doctorates. Of the 352 combined degrees, 129 (36.7%) are doctorates, 92 (26.1%) are master's, 76 (21.6%) are bachelor's, 30

(8.5%) are Juris Doctor degrees (JD), 21 (6%) are doctor of medicine degrees (MD), and 4 (1.1%) are associate degrees. Of the 129 doctorate degrees, 117 (90.7%) are Ph.Ds.

Of the 352 combined degrees, 259 (73.6%) were earned by men and 93 (26.4%) by women. Men earned 107 (30.4% of the total 352 degrees), and women earned 22 (6.3%) of the doctorate degrees; men earned 60 (17.1%), and women earned 32 (9.1%) of the master's degrees; men earned 54 (15.3%), and women earned 22 (6.3%) of the bachelor's degrees; men earned 19 (5.4%), and women earned 11 (3.1%) of the doctor of medicine degrees; men earned 16 (4.6%), and women earned 5 (1.4%) of the doctor of medicine degrees; and men earned 3 (0.9%), and women earned 1 (0.9%) of the associate degrees.

For the various racial groups, Whites earned 230 (65.3%) degrees (163 for men and 67 for women), 88 (25% of the total 352 degrees) of the 129 doctorates (72 men and 16 women), 55 (15.6% of the total 352 degrees) of the master's degrees (32 men and 23 women), 52 (14.8% of the total 352 degrees) of the bachelor's degrees (35 men and 17 women), 17 (4.8% of the total 352 degrees) of Juris Doctor degrees (11 men and 6 women), 15 (4.3% of the total 352 degrees) doctor of medicine degrees (10 men and 5 women), and 3 (0.9% of the total 352 degrees) of the 4 associate degrees (all three by men). Asians earned 100 (28.4%) of the total 352 degrees (76 men and 24 women); 35 (9.9% of the total 352 degrees) doctorate degrees (29 men and 6 women), 32 (9.1% of the total 352 degrees) master's degrees (24 men and 8 women), 14 (4% of the total 352 degrees) bachelor's degrees (10 men and 4 women); 12 (3.4% of the total 352 degrees) Juris Doctor degrees (7 men and 5 women), 6 (1.7% of the total 352 degrees) doctor of medicine degrees (all by men), and 1 (0.3% of total 352 degrees) earned an associate degree (a woman). Blacks earned 21 (6% of the total 352 degrees) degrees (19 men and 2 women): 9 (2.6% of the total 352 degrees) bachelor's degrees (8 men and 1 women), 6 (1.7% of the total 352 degrees) doctorate degrees (all by men), 5 (1.4% of total degrees) master's degrees (4 men and 1 woman), and 1 earned 1 (0.3% of the total 352 degrees) Juris Doctor degree (a man). Finally, 1 (0.3% of total 352 degrees) American Indian male earned a bachelor's degree (Table 8).

Table 8. Levels and Types of Earned Highest/Terminal Higher Education Degrees by Carnegie Corporation of New York's "Pride of America" Honorees, by Race and Sex, 2006-2015

n= 352 degrees and 323 honorees (27 honorees have 2 or more degrees, for a total of 29 extra degrees. When those 29 extra degrees are subtracted from the total of 352, there are 323 honorees with 352 total degrees. Please see note below).

Degree Type	All #	Men #	% of Total	Women #	% of Total	White #	% of Total	White Men #	% of Total	White Women #	% of Total	Asian #	% of Total	Asian Men #	% of Total	Asian Women #	% of Total	Black #	% of Total	Black Men #	% of Total	Black Women #	% of Total	AI Men #	% of Total
Associate/Diploma	4	3	75	1	25	3	75	3	75	..	..	1	25	..	..	1	25	..	..	..	..	..	..	..	..
Bachelor's	76	54	71.1	22	28.9	52	68.4	35	46	17	22.4	14	18.4	10	13.2	4	5.3	9	11.8	8	10.5	1	1.3	1	1.3
Master's	92	60	65.2	32	34.8	55	59.8	32	34.8	23	25	32	34.8	24	26.1	8	8.7	5	5.4	4	4.4	1	1.1	..	..
Doctorate	129	107	83	22	17	88	68.2	72	55.8	16	12.4	35	27.1	29	22.5	6	4.7	6	4.7	6	4.7	..	..	..	..
Ph.D.	117	97	82.9	20	20.6	82	70.1	67	57.3	15	12.8	30	25.6	25	21.4	5	4.3	5	3.9	5	3.9	..	..	..	..
D.Phil.	2	1	50	1	50	2	100	1	50	1	50	..	..	..	..	..	..	..	..	..	..	..	..	..	..
DMA	3	2	66.7	1	33.3	..	..	..	..	..	..	3	100	2	66.7	1	33.3	..	..	..	..	..	..	..	..
Sc.D.	4	4	100	..	..	1	25	1	25	..	..	2	50	2	50	..	..	1	25	1	25	..	..	..	..
Dr. iur. utr.	1	1	100	..	..	1	100	1	100	..	..	..	..	..	..	..	..	..	..	..	..	..	..	..	..
Doctoral Degree	1	1	100	..	..	1	100	1	100	..	..	..	..	..	..	..	..	..	..	..	..	..	..	..	..
Dr. med	1	1	100	..	..	1	100	1	100	..	..	..	..	..	..	..	..	..	..	..	..	..	..	..	..
JD	30	19	63.3	11	36.7	17	56.7	11	36.7	6	20	12	40	7	23.3	5	16.7	1	3.3	1	3.3	..	..	..	..
MD	21	16	76.2	5	23.8	15	71.4	10	47.6	5	23.8	6	28.6	6	28.6	..	..	..	..	..	..	..	..	..	..
Total	352	259	73.6	93	26.4	230	65.3	163	46.3	67	19	100	28.4	76	21.6	24	6.8	21	6	19	5.4	2	0.6	1	0.3

Source: Compiled and computed from June 24, 2015, to January 6, 2016, based on data from: "Great Immigrants: The Pride of America". Carnegie Corporation of New York. http://greatimmigrants.carnegie.org/pride-america/.

Note: For bachelor's degrees, 73 honorees earned 76 bachelor's degrees: 3 honorees (2 White men and 1 White women) have 2

bachelor's degrees each. For master's, 80 honorees earned 92 master's degrees: 1 White man earned 3 master's degrees; 2 White men earned 2 master's degrees each; 4 White women earned 2 master's degrees each; 1 Asian man earned 3 master's degrees; and 2 Asian men earned 2 master's degrees each. For doctoral degrees, 128 honorees earned 129 doctoral degrees: There is 1 White man with 2 doctoral degrees;
Note: AI= American Indian

Academic Major of Earned Highest/Terminal Higher Education Degrees Earned by Carnegie Corporation of New York's "Pride of America" Honorees, by Race and Sex, 2006-2015

An attempt to find the academic majors of the 352 earned degrees was made in this study. This is especially important because one could find some similarities or differences between foreign-born and native-born individuals in the United States in terms of college majors. As Tables 11 and 13 will show later, the vast majority of the honorees earned their highest or terminal degrees from colleges and universities in the United States. For example, the "Selected Fields of Study" of international students in U.S. colleges and universities during the 2014-2015 academic year are as follows: Business and Management (197,258 or 20.2%), Engineering (196,750 or 20.2%), Math and Computer Science (112,950 or 11.6%), Social Sciences (75,951 or 7.8%), Physical and Life Sciences (73,838 or 7.6%), Fine and Applied Arts (56,758 or 5.8%), Intensive English (49,233 or 5%), Health Professions (33,399 or 3.4%), Communications and Journalism (20,161 or 2.1%), Education (17,675 or 1.8%), Humanities (17,504 or 1.8%), Legal Studies and Law Enforcement (13,778 or 1.4%), and Agriculture (12,278 or 1.3%). STEM (Science, Technology, Engineering and Mathematics) fields accounted for 44% of all enrollments ("International Students in the U.S.: 2015 "Fast Facts,'" 2016). According to Han et al. (2015), "Approximately one third of science and engineering post-graduate students in the United States are foreign-born, with particular concentrations in computer science and physics…" (p.2).

Pertaining to degree attainment, of the 12,504 doctorate degrees earned in the Life Sciences in 2014 in the United States, U.S. citizens and permanent residents accounted for 8,438 (67.5%) of them. Temporary visa holders accounted for 3,156 or 25.2%, and "Unknown" accounted for 910 or 7.3 percent " Of the 9,859 doctorate degrees earned in the Physical Sciences in 2014, U.S. citizens and permanent residents accounted for 5,061 (51.3%) of them, temporary visa holders accounted for 4,094 or 41.5%, and "Unknown" accounted for 704 or 7.1 percent. Of the 8,657 doctorate degrees earned in the Social Sciences in 2014, U.S. citizens and permanent residents accounted for 6,268 (72.4%) of them; temporary visa holders accounted for 1,553 or 17.9%, and "Unknown" accounted for 836 or 9.7 percent. Of the 9,568 doctorate degrees earned in Engineering in 2014, U.S. citizens and permanent resident accounted for 4,029 (42.1%) of them, temporary visa holders accounted for 4,936 or 51.6%, and "Unknown" accounted for 603 or 6.3 percent. Of the 4,793 doctorate degrees earned in Education in 2014, U.S. citizens and permanent residents accounted for 3,931 (82%) of them, temporary visa holders accounted for 478 or 10%; and 384 or 8% for "Unknown." Finally, of the 5,486 doctorate degrees earned in the Humanities in 2014, U.S. citizens and permanent resident accounted for 4,360 (79.5%); temporary visa holders for 705 or 12.9%, and "Unknown" accounted for 421 or 7.7% ("TABLE 17. Doctorate recipients, by citizenship status" 2016). These doctorate degree attainment figures show that international students earned a substantial proportion of their doctorates in STEM fields, just as over 4 out of every 10 of them enroll in STEM fields. As Han et al. (2015) note: "… approximately 40% of science and engineering post-graduate students in the United States are foreign-born…" (pp.2-3).

Table 9 presents the various academic majors of the degrees earned by the "Pride of America" honorees. According to Table 9, of the 4 associate degrees earned, academic majors are available for only 3: Music (2 White men) and Fashion Design (1 Asian woman). There are 75 bachelor's degrees earned in 49 academic majors, with a number of majors interrelated. The academic majors with 3 or more bachelor's degrees are Business Administration/Management and Fine Arts each, (5); Economics and Physics each, (4); Communications, Engineering, and Mathematics each, (3). Men earned 2 or more bachelor's degrees in Physics, (4); Business Administration/Management, Economics, Fine Arts, each (3); and Computer Science, Computer Science and Mathematics, English, Mathematics, "Philosophy, Politics and Economics," and Theatre each, (2); women earned 2 bachelor's degrees each in Business Administration/Management, Communications, and Fine Arts. For a racial breakdown, Whites earned more than 2 bachelor's degrees in the following subjects: Fine Arts, 3 (1 man and 2 women), and Physics, 3 (all by men). Asians earned 2 bachelor's degrees or more in Economics, 2 (1 man and 1 woman). Blacks earned 2 bachelor's degrees or more in Business Administration/Management, 2 (1 man and 1 woman). Finally, the American Indian male honoree earned a bachelor's degree in Mathematics.

For master's degrees, I identified 91 degrees earned in 37 academic majors. The following majors have 3 or more master's degrees: Business Administration/Management, 20 (19 men and 1 woman); Fine Arts, 11 (6 men and 5 women); Engineering 7 (5 men and 2 women); International Relations/Affairs/Studies, 5 (3 men and 2 women); Journalism, 5 (3 women and 2 men); Architecture, 4 (3 men and 1 woman); Computer Science, 3 (2 men and 1 woman); and Public Administration/ Affairs, 3 (2 women and 1 man). For a racial breakdown, Whites earned 3 or more master's degrees in the following subjects: Business Administration/Management, 11 (all men); Engineering, 4 (3 men and 1 woman); Fine Arts, 4 (3 women and 1 man); International Relations/Affairs/Studies, 4 (2 men and 2 women); Architecture, 3 (all men); Journalism, 3 (all women). Asians earned 2 degrees or more in the following subjects: Business Administration/Management, 8 (7 men and 1 woman); Engineering, 3 (2 men and 1 woman); Fine Arts, 3 (2 men and 1 woman); Computer Science, 2 (1 man and 1 woman); Journalism, 2 (both men); and Public Administration/Affairs, 2 (1 man and 1 woman). Finally, Blacks earned 4 master's degrees in Fine Arts (3 men and 1 woman) and 1 master's degree in Business Administration/Management (a man).

For doctorate degrees, 129 degrees were earned in 48 academic majors. The following majors have 4 or more doctorate degrees: Engineering, 18 (17 men and 1 woman); Physics, 13 (all men); Economics, 10 (all men); Chemistry, 8 (7 men and 1 woman); Physics, 8 (all men); Biochemistry, 6 (5 men and 1 woman); History, 5 (3 women and 2 by men); Biology, 4 (3 women and 1 man); and Business Administration/Management and Political Science each, 4 (all men). For a racial breakdown, Whites earned 3 or more doctorate degrees in the following subjects: Engineering, 13 (12 men and 1 woman); Economics, 8 (all men); Chemistry, 6 (all men); Biochemistry, 5 (4 men and 1 woman); History, 4 (3 women and 1 man); and Political Science, 4 (all men). For Asians, 2 or more doctorate degrees are earned in the following subjects: Physics, 5 (all men); Business Administration/ Management and Engineering each, 3 (all men); Biology, 2 (1 man and 1 woman); Chemistry, 2 (1 man and 1 woman); and Music, 2 (all men). Finally, for Blacks, all 6 doctorate degrees are earned by men in the following subjects: Economics and Engineering each, 2; History, 1; and Sociology, 1 (Table 9).

Table 9. Academic Major of Earned Highest/Terminal Higher Education Degrees of Carnegie Corporation of New York's "Pride of America" Honorees, by Race and Sex, 2006-2015

Associate Degree n=4	All	Men	Women	White	White Men	White Women	Asian	Asian Men	Asian Women	Black	Black Men	Black Women	AI Men
Academic Major n=3 majors	#	#	#	#	#	#	#	#	#	#	#	#	#
Music	2	2		2	2								
Fashion Design	1		1				1		1				
Total	3	2	1	2	2	0	1	0	1				
Bachelor's Degree n=75													
Academic Major n=49													
Accounting	1	1		1	1								
Acting	1	1		1	1								
Architecture	1	1		1	1								
Business Administration/Management	5	3	2	2	1	1	1	1		2	1	1	
Business Administration/ International Marketing	1	1		1	1								
Chemistry	1		1	1		1							
Clinical Hypnotherapy	1		1	1		1							
Clothing Merchandising	1		1	1		1							
Commerce	1		1	1		1							
Communications	3	1	2	2		2				1	1		
Computer Science	2	2		1	1		1	1					
Computer Science & Mathematics	2	2		1	1		1	1					
Creative Writing	1	1								1	1		
Culture & Media	1	1		1	1								
Dramatic Studies	1	1		1	1								
Economics	4	3	1	2	2		2	1	1				
Education	1	1		1	1								

Table 9 continues...

Associate Degree n=4	All	Men	Women	White	White Men	White Women	Asian	Asian Men	Asian Women	Black	Black Men	Black Women	AI Men
Academic Major n=3 majors	#	#	#	#	#	#	#	#	#	#	#	#	#
English	2	2		1	1		1	1					
English & French Literature	1	1		1	1								
English & History	1	1		1	1								
English Language & Literature/Letters	1		1				1		1				
English Literature	1	1		1	1								
Ethics, History, English & Psychology	1		1				1		1				
Fashion Design	1		1				1		1				
Fine Arts	5	3	2	3	1	2	1	1		1	1		
Geology	1	1		1	1								
German Language & Culture	1		1	1		1							
History	1	1								1	1		
Hotel & Restaurant Management	1	1								1	1		
Humanities	1		1	1		1							
Journalism	1	1		1	1								
Latin American Studies & Political Economy	1		1	1		1							
Liberal Arts	1	1					1	1					
Linguistics & Diplomacy	1	1								1	1		
Literature & Art History	1	1		1	1								
Management Information System	1	1		1	1								
Mathematics	3	2	1	2	1	1							1
Music	1	1		1	1								
Philosophy	1	1		1	1								
Philosophy, Politics & Economics	2	2		2	2								
Photojournalism	1		1	1		1							
Physics	4	4		3	3		1	1					
Political Science	2	1	1	1		1				1	1		

Table 9 continues…

Associate Degree n=4	All	Men	Women	White	White Men	White Women	Asian	Asian Men	Asian Women	Black	Black Men	Black Women	AI Men
Academic Major n=3 majors	#	#	#	#	#	#	#	#	#	#	#	#	#
Political Science & Public Administration	1		1	1		1							
Psychology	1		1	1		1							
Russian Literature	1	1		1	1								
Theatre	2	2		1	1		1	1					
Urban Studies	1	1		1	1								
Total	75	53	22	51	34	17	14	10	4	9	8	1	1
Master's Degree n=91													
Academic Major n=37													
Acting	1	1					1	1					
Aeronautical Science	1	1		1	1								
American Government	1	1		1	1								
Anaerobic Microbiology	1		1	1		1							
Applied Mathematics & Computer Science	1	1		1	1								
Architecture	4	3	1	3	3		1	1					
Business Administration/Management	20	19	1	11	11		8	7	1	1	1		
City Planning	1		1	1		1							
Communications	1		1	1		1							
Computer Science	3	2	1	1	1		2	1	1				
Creative Writing	2	1	1	2	1	1							
Economics	2		2	2		2							
Economics & Politics of Development	1		1				1		1				
Engineering	7	5	2	4	3	1	3	2	1				
Film Production	1	1					1	1					
Finance	1		1	1		1							
Fine Arts	11	6	5	4	1	3	3	2	1	4	3	1	
Food Science	1	1					1	1					

Table 9 continues…

Associate Degree n=4	All	Men	Women	White	White Men	White Women	Asian	Asian Men	Asian Women	Black	Black Men	Black Women	AI Men
Academic Major n=3 majors	#	#	#	#	#	#	#	#	#	#	#	#	#
History	1	1		1	1								
Information Systems Management	1	1					1	1					
International Relations/Affairs/Studies	5	3	2	4	2	2	1	1					
Interpretation	1		1	1		1							
Journalism	5	2	3	3		3	2	2					
Law	1	1		1	1								
Law and Diplomacy	1		1				1		1				
Library Science	1	1					1	1					
Literature	2		2	2		2							
Management	2		2	1		1	1		1				
Mass Communications Research & Political Science	1	1		1	1								
Music	1	1					1	1					
National Security & Strategic Studies	1	1					1	1					
Politics, Ethics & Economics	1	1		1	1								
Psychology	1	1		1	1								
Public Administration/Affairs	3	1	2	1		1	2	1	1				
Social Work	1	1		1	1								
Space System Operations	1	1		1	1								
Academic Major n=3 majors	#	#	#	#	#	#	#	#	#	#	#	#	#
Spanish	1	1		1	1								
Total	91	60	31	54	33	21	32	24	8	5	4	1	
Doctorate Degree n=129													
Academic Major n=48													
Anthropology	2	1	1	1		1	1	1					

Table 9 continues…

Associate Degree n=4	All	Men	Women	White	White Men	White Women	Asian	Asian Men	Asian Women	Black	Black Men	Black Women	AI Men
Academic Major n=3 majors	#	#	#	#	#	#	#	#	#	#	#	#	#
Architecture	1		1	1		1							
Art	1	1		1	1								
Astrophysics	2	2		2	2								
Biochemistry	6	5	1	5	4	1	1	1					
Biology	4	1	3	2		2	2	1	1				
Biology/Biochemistry	1	1					1	1					
Biophysics	1	1		1	1								
Business Administration/ Management	4	4		1	1		3	3					
Chemistry	8	7	1	6	6		2	1	1				
Comparative Literature	2	1	1	2	1	1							
Computer Science	3	3		2	2		1	1					
Economics	10	10		8	8					2	2		
Engineering	18	17	1	13	12	1	3	3		2	2		
English & American Literature	1	1					1	1					
English Literature	1		1	1		1							
Experimental Medicine	1	1		1	1								
Finance	1	1					1	1					
Genetics	1	1					1	1					
Geology	1	1		1	1								
Government	2	2		1	1		1	1					
Higher Education	1		1	1		1							
History	5	2	3	4	1	3				1	1		
International Relations	3	2	1	2	2		1		1				
Law	1	1		1	1								
Letters	1	1		1	1								
Linguistics	2	2		1	1		1	1					

Table 9 continues...

Associate Degree n=4	All	Men	Women	White	White Men	White Women	Asian	Asian Men	Asian Women	Black	Black Men	Black Women	AI Men
Academic Major n=3 majors	#	#	#	#	#	#	#	#	#	#	#	#	#
Logic	1	1		1	1								
Material Science & Engineering	2	2		2	2								
Mathematics	3	2	1	2	1	1	1	1					
Microsurgery	1		1	1		1							
Music	3	3		1	1		2	2					
Oncology	1	1		1	1								
Organizational Behavior	1	1					1	1					
Philosophy	1	1		1	1								
Physics	13	13		8	8		5	5					
Physics and Mathematics	1	1		1	1								
Political Science	4	4		4	4								
Political Science/Public Admin.	1		1				1		1				
Psychology	2	2		1	1		1	1					
Public Law & Government	1		1	1		1							
Renaissance Studies	1		1				1		1				
Sociology	3	3		1	1		1	1		1	1		
Statistics	1	1					1	1					
Technical Sciences	2	2		2	2								
Violin	1		1				1		1				
Virology	1	1		1	1								
Zoology	1		1	1		1							
Total	129	107	22	88	72	16	35	29	6	6	6		

Source: Compiled and computed from June 24, 2015, to January 6, 2016, based on data from: "Great Immigrants: The Pride of America". Carnegie Corporation of New York. http://greatimmigrants.carnegie.org/pride-america/.

Year of Graduation from Higher Education Institutions by Carnegie Corporation of New York's "Pride of America" Honorees, by Race and Sex, 2006-2015

Table 10 presents available year of graduation data for "Pride of America" honorees with earned higher education degrees. This aggregate data helps to provide a better understanding of their educational attainment. According to Table 10, of the 4 associate degrees earned by 4 honorees, 2 were earned in 1969 (both by White men), and 1 was earned in 1976 (White man), and 1 was earned in 1978 (Asian woman). I identified 72 bachelor's degrees earned (53 men and 19 women) in 48 different years, ranging from 1969 to 2014. Three bachelor's degrees or more were earned in the following years: 1997, 6 (5 men and 1 woman); 1992, 4 (3 men and 1 woman); 1985, 3 (all men); and 1979, 3 (2 women and 1 man). Two bachelor's degrees were earned in 12 different years. For a racial breakdown, 48 bachelor's degrees were earned by Whites (34 men and 14 women): 4 bachelor's degrees in 1997 (3 men and 1 woman) and 3 bachelor's degrees in 1992 (2 men and 1women); 2 degrees by men in 7 different years (1949, 1950, 1955, 1966, 1970, 1985, and 1992), but only in one year (1984) for women. For Asians, 14 bachelor's degrees were earned (10 by men and 4 by women), including 2 degrees (all men) earned in 1997. For Blacks, 9 bachelor's degrees were earned (8 men and 1 woman), including 2 degrees earned (all men) in 1999. One bachelor's degree was earned by an American Indian male honoree in 1972.

For master's degrees, I identified 87 honorees who earned them in 49 different years (55 men and 32 women), ranging from 1946 to 2015. Three or more master's degrees were earned in the following years: 5 in 1990 (4 men and 1 woman), 4 in 1993 (2 men and 2 women), 3 each in 1962 (all men), 1965 (2 men and 1 woman), 1973 (2 women and 1 man), 1978 (2 men and 1 woman), 1984 (2 men and 1 woman), and 1992 (2 men and 1 woman). For a racial breakdown, I identified 53 master's degrees earned by Whites (30 men and 23 women), 3 in 1965 (2 men and 1 woman), and 2 degrees each by White men in 6 different years (1953, 1962, 1965, 1988, 1990 and 2006) and by White women in 3 different years (1973, 1974, and 1982). For Asians, 2 or more master's degrees were earned in 1984, 3 (2 men and 1 woman), 3 in 1990 (2 men and 1 woman), 2 in 1980 (1 man and 1 woman), 2 in 1987 (1 man and 1 woman), 2 in 1993 (all men), and 2 in 1995 (1 man and 1 woman). For Blacks, 5 master's degrees were earned; 1 each in 1972, 1995, 2005, and 2015 (all men) and 1 in 1993 (1 woman).

The 30 Juris Doctor degrees were earned in 20 different years by 19 men and 11 women (from 1953 to 2004). Two or more Juris Doctorate degrees were earned in the following years: 3 each in 1974, 1978, and 1995 (each by 2 men and 1 woman) and 2 each in 1960 (each by 1 man and 1 woman), 1966 (1 man and 1 woman), 1993 (all men), and 2000 (1 man and 1 woman). Whites earned 17 Juris Doctor degrees (11 men and 6 women); 2 degrees each in 1966 and 1972 (each by 1 man and 1 woman). Asians earned 12 Juris Doctor degrees (7 men and 5 women); 2 degrees each in 1960, 1978, 1995, and 2000 (each by 1 man and 1 woman), and 1993 (all by men). Finally, one Black man earned a Juris Doctor degree in 1984.

Of the 21 doctor of medicine degrees (16 men and 5 women) earned in 19 different years (from 1945 to 2006), two were earned each in 1975 (all men) and 1979 (1 man and 1 woman). Fifteen Whites earned doctor of medicine degrees (10 men and 5 women), all earning 1 degree each. Six Asian men earned 1 doctor of medicine degree each.

Finally, of the 129 doctorate degrees earned (107 by men and 22 by women) in 56 different years (from 1905 to 2010); 4 or more of them were earned in the following years: 7 in 1993 (6 men and 1 woman); 6 in 1979 (5 men and 1 woman); 5 each in 1948, 1973, 1982, and 1988 (all men), 1977 (4 men and 1 woman); and 4 each in 1964 (all men), 1976 (3 women and 1 man), and 1983 (3 men and 1 woman). Whites earned 88 doctorate degrees (72 men and 16 women): 4 or more in the following years: 5 in 1977 (4 men and 1 woman); and 4 each in 1964 and 1982 (all men), 1979 and 1983 (each by 3 men and 1 woman). Asians earned 35 doctorate degrees (29 men and 6 women): 2 or more in the following years: 7 in 1993 (6 men and 1 woman); 3 each in 1948 (all men) and 2000 (2 by men and 1 woman); and 2 each in 1971, 1976 (all men), and 1972 (all women). Black men earned 6 doctorate degrees in 6 different years: 1973, 1979, 1982, 1985, 1991, and 1994 (Table 10).

Table 10 Year of Graduation from Higher Education Institutions of Carnegie Corporation of New York's "Pride of America" Honorees, by Race and Sex, 2006-2015

Year of Degree Attainment Associate/Diploma (n=4) 3 years	All	Men	Women	White	White Men	White Women	Asian	Asian Men	Asian Women	Black	Black Men	Black Women	AI Men
Year	#	#	#	#	#	#	#	#	#	#	#	#	#
1969	2	2		2	2								
1976	1	1		1	1								
1978	1		1				1		1				
Total	4	3	1	3	3	0	1	0	1				
Bachelor's Degree (n=72) 48 Years													
Year													
1935	1		1	1		1							
1937	1	1		1	1								
1945	1	1		1	1								
1948	1	1		1	1								
1949	2	2		2	2								
1950	2	2		2	2								
1951	1	1		1	1								
1954	1	1		1	1								
1955	2	2		2	2								
1957	1		1				1		1				
1960	1	1		1	1								
1961	1	1		1	1								
1962	1	1		1	1								
1963	1	1		1	1								
1965	1		1	1		1							
1966	2	2		2	2								

Table 10 continues...

Year of Degree Attainment	All	Men	Women	White	White Men	White Women	Asian	Asian Men	Asian Women	Black	Black Men	Black Women	AI
Associate/Diploma (n=4) 3 years													Men
Year	#	#	#	#	#	#	#	#	#	#	#	#	#
1967	1	1		1	1								
1968	2	1	1	1	1		1		1				
1970	2	2		2	2								
1972	1	1											1
1973	1	1		1	1								
1975	2	1	1	1		1	1	1					
1976	2	2		1	1		1	1					
1977	1	1					1	1					
1978	1		1	1		1							
1979	3	1	2	2	1	1	1		1				
1981	1		1	1		1							
1984	2		2	2		2							
1985	3	3		2	2					1	1		
1987	1		1	1		1							
1988	2	2		1	1		1	1					
1989	1	1					1	1					
1990	1		1	1		1							
1991	1	1								1	1		
1992	4	3	1	3	2	1	1	1					
1993	2	2		1	1					1	1		
1994	1		1	1		1							
1995	1		1	1		1							
1996	1	1					1	1					
1997	6	5	1	4	3	1	2	2					
1999	2	2								2	2		
2000	1	1		1	1								
2002	1	1					1	1					

Table 10 continues…

Year of Degree Attainment	All	Men	Women	White	White Men	White Women	Asian	Asian Men	Asian Women	Black	Black Men	Black Women	AI Men
Associate/Diploma (n=4) 3 years													
Year	#	#	#	#	#	#	#	#	#	#	#	#	#
2003	1	1								1	1		
2004	1	1								1	1		
2006	1		1							1	1		
2011	1	1								1		1	
2014	1		1				1		1				
Total	72	53	19	48	34	14	14	10	4	9	8	1	
Master's Degree (n=87) 49 Years													
Year													
1946	1	1					1	1					
1951	1	1		1	1								
1952	1	1		1	1								
1953	2	2		2	2								
1954	1	1		1	1								
1957	1		1	1		1							
1959	2	2		1	1		1	1					
1960	2		2	1		1	1		1				
1961	1	1		1	1								
1962	3	3		2	2		1	1					
1963	1		1	1		1							
1965	3	2	1	3	2	1							
1967	1		1	1		1							
1968	2	2		1	1		1	1					
1970	1	1		1	1								
1971	2	1	1	2	1	1							
1972	2	1	1	1		1				1	1		
1973	3	1	2	2		2	1	1					
1974	2		2	2		2							

Table 10 continues...

Year of Degree Attainment	All	Men	Women	White	White Men	White Women	Asian	Asian Men	Asian Women	Black	Black Men	Black Women	AI
Associate/Diploma (n=4) 3 years													Men
Year	#	#	#	#	#	#	#	#	#	#	#	#	#
1975	2	2		1	1		1	1					
1976	1	1		1	1								
1977	2	1	1	2	1	1							
1978	3	2	1	2	1	1	1	1					
1979	2		2	1		1	1		1				
1980	2	1	1				2	1	1				
1981	1		1	1		1							
1982	2		2	2		2							
1983	1		1	1		1							
1984	3	2	1				3	2	1				
1985	1	1		1	1								
1987	3	1	2	1		1	2	1	1				
1988	2	2		2	2								
1990	5	4	1	2	2		3	2	1				
1991	2		2	1		1	1		1				
1992	3	2	1	2	1	1	1	1					
1993	4	2	2	1		1	2	2		1		1	
1995	3	2	1				2	1	1	1	1		
1996	1	1					1	1					
1997	1	1					1	1					
1999	1	1		1	1								
2001	1	1					1	1					
2002	1	1		1	1								
2003	1		1	1		1							
2004	1	1		1	1								
2005	1	1								1	1		
2006	2	2		2	2								

Table 10 continues...

Year of Degree Attainment	All	Men	Women	White	White Men	White Women	Asian	Asian Men	Asian Women	Black	Black Men	Black Women	AI
Associate/Diploma (n=4) 3 years													Men
Year	#	#	#	#	#	#	#	#	#	#	#	#	#
2008	1	1		1	1								
2010	1	1					1	1					
2015	1	1								1	1		
Total	87	55	32	53	30	23	29	21	8	5	4	1	
Juris Doctor Degree (n=30)													
20 Years													
1953	1	1		1	1								
1958	1	1		1	1								
1960	2	1	1				2	1	1				
1966	2	1	1	2	1	1							
1970	1		1	1		1							
1973	1	1		1	1								
1974	3	2	1	2	1	1	1	1					
1978	3	2	1	1	1		2	1	1				
1984	1	1								1	1		
1985	1	1		1	1								
1986	1		1	1		1							
1987	1		1	1		1							
1992	1	1		1	1								
1993	2	2					2	2					
1994	1	1		1	1								
1995	3	2	1	1	1		2	1	1				
1997	1		1				1		1				
1999	1		1	1		1							
2000	2	1	1				2	1	1				

Table 10 continues...

Year of Degree Attainment	All	Men	Women	White	White Men	White Women	Asian	Asian Men	Asian Women	Black	Black Men	Black Women	AI Men
Associate/Diploma (n=4) 3 years													
Year	#	#	#	#	#	#	#	#	#	#	#	#	#
2004	1	1		1	1								
Total	30	19	11	17	11	6	12	7	5	1	1		
Doctor of Medicine Degree (n=21) 19 years													
Year													
1945	1	1		1	1								
1949	1	1		1	1								
1956	1	1		1	1								
1957	1	1		1	1								
1960	1	1		1	1								
1962	1	1		1	1								
1969	1	1					1	1					
1972	1	1					1	1					
1974	1		1	1		1							
1975	2	2		1	1		1	1					
1978	1	1					1	1					
1979	2	1	1	1		1	1	1					
1980	1		1	1		1							
1982	1	1		1	1								
1984	1		1	1		1							
1991	1	1					1	1					
1993	1	1		1	1								
1999	1	1		1	1								
2006	1		1	1		1							
Total	21	16	5	15	10	5	6	6					
Doctorate Degree													
Year (n=129) 56 years													
1905	1	1		1	1								

Table 10 continues...

Year of Degree Attainment Associate/Diploma (n=4) 3 years	All	Men	Women	White	White Men	White Women	Asian	Asian Men	Asian Women	Black	Black Men	Black Women	AI Men
Year	#	#	#	#	#	#	#	#	#	#	#	#	#
1938	1	1		1	1								
1945	1	1		1	1								
1947	1	1		1	1								
1948	5	5		2	2		3	3					
1949	1	1		1	1		1	1					
1950	2	2		1	1								
1951	1	1		1	1								
1952	1	1					1	1					
1953	3	3		3	3		1						
1954	3	3		2	3								
1956	2	2		3	2								
1957	1		1	1		1							
1960	1	1		1	1								
1962	3	3		3	3								
1963	2	2		1	1				1				
1964	4	4		4	4								
1965	1	1					1	1					
1966	1	1		1	1								
1967	1	1					1	1					
1968	1	1		1	1								
1969	3	2	1	3	2	1							
1970	1	1		1	1								
1971	2	2					2	2					
1972	3	1	2	1	1		2		2				
1973	5	5		3	3		1	1		1	1		
1974	1	1		1	1								

Table 10 continues...

Year of Degree Attainment	All	Men	Women	White	White Men	White Women	Asian	Asian Men	Asian Women	Black	Black Men	Black Women	AI
Associate/Diploma (n=4) 3 years													Men
Year	#	#	#	#	#	#	#	#	#	#	#	#	#
1975	1		1	1		1							
1976	4	3	1	2	1	1	2	2					
1977	5	4	1	5	4	1							
1978	2	2		2	2								
1979	6	5	1	4	3	1	1	1		1	1		
1980	3	1	2	2		2	1	1					
1981	3	3		2	2		1	1					
1982	5	5		4	4					1	1		
1983	4	3	1	4	3	1							
1984	1	1		1	1								
1985	3	1	2	1		1	1		1	1	1		
1986	2	2		1	1		1	1					
1987	3	3		3	3								
1988	4	4		3	3		1	1					
1991	3	3		2	2					1	1		
1992	3	3		3	3								
1993	7	6	1				7	6	1				
1994	1	1								1	1		
1996	1	1		1	1								
1997	2	1	1	1	1		1		1				
1998	2	1	1	1		1	1	1					
1999	2	2		1	1		1	1					
2000	3	2	1				3	2	1				
2002	2	1	1	1		1	1	1					
2003	1		1	1		1							

Table 10 continues...

Year of Degree													
Attainment	All	Men	Women	White	White Men	White Women	Asian	Asian Men	Asian Women	Black	Black Men	Black Women	AI
Associate/Diploma (n=4) 3 years													Men
Year	#	#	#	#	#	#	#	#	#	#	#	#	#
2004	1		1	1		1							
2005	1		1	1		1							
2009	1	1		1	1								
2010	1		1	1		1							
Total	129	107	22	88	72	16	35	29	6	6	6		

Source: Compiled and computed from June 24, 2015, to January 6, 2016, based on data from: "Great Immigrants: The Pride of America". Carnegie Corporation of New York. http://greatimmigrants.carnegie.org/pride-america/.

Academic Institutions where Highest/Terminal Higher Education Degrees are earned by Carnegie Corporation of New York's "Pride of America" Honorees, by Race and Sex, 2006-2015

Most successful immigrants in the United States attended or graduated from the country's higher education institutions, including many of its most selective and highly ranked institutions. No and Walsh (2010) point out in their study on inventors in the United States that those born abroad earned their terminal or highest higher education degrees in the United States: "… but a significant minority (over 30%) was educated overseas. Inventors born outside of the US are also much more likely to have a PhD (68% versus 37%...)" (p.290). Young (2015) claims that two of the immigrants who won Nobel Prizes for the United States in October 2015 (William Campbell and Aziz Sancar) earned their terminal degrees in the United States and decided to stay and work there to help train young scientists. Speaking of Aziz Sancar: "He came on a visa to the United States to earn his Ph.D. and stayed afterwards to do groundbreaking research. Both men devoted much of their later lives to training younger scientists."

Table 11 supports the claims made above by illustrating that the vast majority of the "Pride of America" honorees earned their highest or terminal degrees from colleges and universities in the United States, including many of its leading institutions. Thirteen of the institutions listed below, were among the top 20 hosts of international students during the 2014-2015 academic year - among them New York University (#1, 13,178 students); the University of Southern California (#2, 12,334 students); Columbia University (#3, 11,510 students); the University of Illinois, Urbana-Champaign (#5, 11,223 students); Purdue University, West Lafayette (#7, 10,230 students); the University of California, Los Angeles (#8, 10,209 students); Michigan State University (#9, 8,146 students); and the University of Washington (#10, 8,035 students) ("International Students in the U.S.," 2016).

According to Table 11, those honorees who earned their degrees abroad did so at leading institutions. According to Table 11, the four associate degrees were received at Hong Kong Polytechnic, Julliard School, Mannes College of Music, and George Washington University respectively. The study identified 73 bachelor's degrees earned at 58 higher education institutions (53 men and 20 women). Two or more bachelor's degrees were earned at 12 institutions: 4 from the University of Oxford (all men); 3 from the University of Texas, Austin (2 women and 1 man) and 2 each from California State University, Los Angeles, Columbia University, Florida International University, Julliard School, the University of Miami (1 man and 1 woman each), City University of New York, New York University, the University of Pennsylvania, the University of Southern California, and Yale University (all men). For a racial breakdown, Whites earned 50 (68.5%) of the 73 bachelor's degrees (35 men and 15 women); 2 or more degrees from the following 9 institutions: 4 at the University of Oxford (all men); 2 each from Columbia University, Florida International University, Julliard School, and the University of Miami (1 man and 1 woman each), the University of Pennsylvania, the University of Southern California, and Yale University (all men). Asians earned 1 bachelor's degree each from 14 different institutions (10 men and 4 women). Blacks earned 1 bachelor's degree each from 8 different institutions (7 men and 1 women). Finally, 1 American Indian male honoree earned a bachelor's degree from California State University, Los Angeles.

For master's degrees, 92 were earned from 53 institutions (61 by men and 31by women). Three or more degrees were earned from the following 9 institutions; 8 from Columbia University (6 by men and 2 by women), 7 each from Harvard University (6 by men and 1 woman) and Stanford University (4 by men and 3 by women), 5 from New York University (all men), 4 from the University of Pennsylvania (2 by men and 2 by women), 3 each from George Washington University and the University of California, Berkeley (2 by women and 1 man), the Naval Postgraduate School (all men), and the University of Chicago (all men). Whites earned 55 (59.8%) of the 92 master's degrees (32 by men and 23 by women); 3 or more master's degrees from the following 7 institutions; 5 from Columbia University (3 men and 2 women); 4 from Stanford University (3 by women and 1 man), the University of Pennsylvania (2 by men and 2 by women); 3 each from George Washington University (2 by women and 1 man), Harvard University and the Naval Postgraduate School (all men), and the University of California, Berkeley (2 by women and 1 man). Asians earned 32 master's degrees (24 by men and 8 by women): 2 or more master's degrees from the following institutions: 4 from Harvard University (3 by men and 1 woman), 3 each from New York University and Stanford

University (all men), and 2 from Columbia University (all men). Five Blacks earned master's degrees from 5 institutions (4 by men and 1 woman): Brown University (1 woman), and Columbia University, Cornell University, Hollins University, and the University of Chicago (1 man each).

All 30 Juris Doctor degrees (19 men and 11 women) were earned from 24 institutions. Two or more were earned from 3 institutions: 4 from Harvard University (2 men and 2 women), 3 from Columbia University (2 men and 1 woman), and 2 from Stanford University (all men). Whites earned 17 degrees (11 men and 6 women) from 15 institutions: 3 from Harvard University (2 women and 1 man). Asians earned 12 degrees (7 men and 5 women) from 11 institutions, with 2 from Columbia University (1 man and 1 woman). One Black man earned a Juris Doctor degree from Columbia University.

All 21 doctor of medicine degrees (16 men and 5 women) were earned from 18 institutions, with 4 from Harvard University (3 men and 1 woman), and 1 each from 17 other institutions. Whites earned 15 doctor of medicine degrees (10 men and 2 women) from 14 institutions, with 2 from Harvard University (1 man and 1 woman). Finally, 6 Asian men earned doctor of medicine degrees from 5 institutions: Harvard University (2) and from the All India Institute of Medical Sciences, Madras Medical College, McGill University, and the University of the Witwatersrand (1 each).

Finally, all of the 129 doctorate degrees (107 by men and 22 by women) were earned from 69 institutions, with 3 or more of them earned from 9 institutions: 14 from Harvard University (11 by men and 3 by women); 10 from the Massachusetts Institute of Technology (9 by men and 1 woman); 8 from the University of California, Berkeley (7 by men and 1 woman); 6 from Columbia University (5 by men and 1 woman); 5 each from Princeton University (4 by men and 1 woman) and the University of Chicago (all men); 4 from the University of Pennsylvania (3 by women and 1 man); 3 from the University of Cambridge (2 by women and 1 man); and 3 from Stanford University (all men). Whites earned 88 doctorate degrees (72 by men and 16 by women), with 3 or more degrees earned from 6 institutions: 9 from Harvard University (6 by men and 3 by women); 7 from the Massachusetts Institute of Technology (6 by men and 1 woman); 5 from the University of California, Berkeley (all men); 4 from Princeton

University (3 by men and 1 woman); 3 from the University of Cambridge (2 by women and 1 man); and 3 from the University of Pennsylvania (all men). Asians earned 35 doctorate degrees (29 by men and 6 by women), with 2 or more degrees from 5 institutions: 5 from Harvard University (all men); 4 from Columbia University (all men); 3 from the University of Chicago (all men); and 2 each from the Massachusetts Institute of Technology (all men) and the University of California, Berkeley (1 man and 1 woman). Finally, Black men earned 6 doctorate degrees from the following 6 institutions: American University, Dalhousie University, the Massachusetts Institute of Technology, the New School for Social Research, the University of Washington, and the University of California, Berkeley (1 each) (Table 11).

Table 11. Academic Institutions Where Highest/Terminal Higher Education Degrees Were Earned by Carnegie Corporation of New York's "Pride of America" Honorees, by Race and Sex, 2006-2015

Academic Institution	All	Men	Women	White	Men	Women	Asian	Men	Women	Black	Men	Women	AI Man
Associate Degree (n=4) 4 Institutions	#	#	#	#	#	#	#	#	#	#	#	#	#
George Washington University	1	1		1									
Hong Kong Polytechnic	1		1										
Julliard School	1	1		1			1		1				
Mannes College of Music	1	1		1									
Total	4	3	1	3			1		1				
Bachelor's Degree (n=73) 58 Institutions													
Binghamton University	1	1					1	1					
Boston University	1	1					1	1					
Brown University	1	1					1	1					
California Institute of the Arts	1		1	1		1							
California State University, Los Angeles	2	1	1	1		1							1

Table 11 continues…

Academic Institution	All	Men	Women	White	Men	Women	Asian	Men	Women	Black	Men	Women	AI Man
Carleton University	1	1		1	1								
City University of New York	2	2		1	1					1	1		
Colgate University	1	1								1	1		
Columbia University	2	1	1	2	1	1							
Dongseo University	1	1					1	1					
Florida International University	2	1	1	2	1	1							
Georgetown University	1	1								1	1		
Harvard University	1	1					1	1					
Institute of Technology, Illinois	1	1		1	1								
Julliard School	2	1	1	2	1	1							
Kinnaird College for Women	1		1				1		1				
Manhattanville College	1		1				1		1				
Middlebury College	1	1		1	1								
New York Institute of Technology	1		1	1		1							
New York University	2	2		1	1		1	1					
Northern Arizona University	1	1								1	1		
Norwegian Institute of Technology	1	1		1	1								
Oberlin College	1	1								1	1		
Oakland City College	1	1		1	1								
Parsons the New School for Design	1		1				1		1				
Princeton University	1		1				1		1				
Queen's University of Belfast	1	1		1	1								
Richmond College	1	1		1	1								
Rosemont College	1		1	1		1							
Royal Academy of Dramatic Art	1	1		1	1								
Royal Scottish Academy of Music & Drama	1	1		1	1								
San Jose State University	1		1	1		1							

Findings/Results and Analysis

Table 11 continues…

Academic Institution	All	Men	Women	White	Men	Women	Asian	Men	Women	Black	Men	Women	AI Man
Sorbonne	1		1	1		1							
Stanford University	1		1	1		1							
Troy State University	1	1								1	1		
Tufts University	1	1		1	1								
University College Dublin	1	1		1	1								
University of California, Berkeley	1	1					1	1					
University of California, Los Angeles	1	1								1	1		
University of Cambridge	1	1		1	1								
University of Cape Town	1	1		1	1								
University of Illinois	1	1					1	1					
University of Maryland, College Park	1	1		1	1								
University of Miami	2	1	1	2	1	1							
University of Minnesota, Duluth	1		1	1		1							
University of Natal	1		1	1		1							
University of Ottawa	1	1		1	1								
University of Oxford	4	4		4	4								
University of Pennsylvania	2	2		2	2								
University of South Florida	1	1					1	1					
University of Southern California	2	2		2	2								
University of Texas, Arlington	1	1					1	1					
University of Texas, Austin	3	1	2	2	1	1				1		1	
University of Toronto	1	1		1	1								
University of Wisconsin, Superior	1	1		1	1								
Washington State University	1	1		1	1								
Western Kentucky University	1		1	1		1							
Yale University	2	2		2	2								
Total	73	53	20	50	35	15	14	10	4	8	7	1	1

Table 11 continues…

Academic Institution	All	Men	Women	White	Men	Women	Asian	Men	Women	Black	Men	Women	AI Man
Master's Degree (n=92) 53 Institutions													
Brown University	1		1							1		1	
Carnegie Mellon University	1	1					1	1					
City University of New York	1	1		1	1								
Columbia University	8	6	2	5	3	2	2	2		1	1		
Cornell University	2	1	1				1		1	1	1		
Durham University	1	1		1	1								
Embry-Riddle Aeronautical University	1	1		1	1								
Fordham University	1		1	1		1							
Georgia Institute of Technology	1	1		1	1								
George Washington University	3	1	2	3	1	2							
Harvard University	7	6	1	3	3		4	3	1				
Hollins University	1	1								1	1		
Institute of Fine Arts	1		1	1		1							
Johns Hopkins University	2		2	2		2							
Massachusetts Institute of Technology	1	1		1	1								
Michigan State University	1	1		1	1								
Middlebury College	1	1		1	1								
Moscow State University	1	1		1	1								
Naval Postgraduate School	3	3		3	3								
New York University	5	5		2	2		3	3					
Our Lady of Lake	1	1		1	1								
Roosevelt University	1	1		1	1								
Salve Regina University	1	1					1	1					
School of the Art Institute of Chicago	1		1				1		1				
Southern New Hampshire University	1	1					1	1					
Stanford University	7	4	3	4	1	3	3	3					

Table 11 continues…

Academic Institution	All	Men	Women	White	Men	Women	Asian	Men	Women	Black	Men	Women	AI Man
Tufts University	1		1				1		1				
United States College of Naval Command and Staff	1	1					1	1					
University of California, Berkeley	3	1	2	3	1	2							
University of California, Davis	1	1					1	1					
University of California, Los Angeles	1	1					1	1					
University of Cambridge	2		2	1		1	1		1				
University of Chicago	3	3		1	1		1	1		1	1		
University of Denver	1	1					1	1					
University of Geneva	1		1	1		1							
University of Illinois	2	1	1	1	1		1		1				
University of Maryland, College Park	1		1	1		1							
University of Maryland, University College	1	1					1	1					
University of Miami	1	1		1	1								
University of Minnesota	1		1	1		1							
University of North Carolina, Charlotte	1	1		1	1								
University of Oregon	1	1					1	1					
University of Ottawa	1	1		1		1							
University of Pennsylvania	4	2	2	4	2	2							
University of Southern California	1		1	1		1							
University of Texas, Austin	1		1				1		1				
University of Vermont	1		1	1		1							
University of Wisconsin, Milwaukee	1	1					1	1					
Vanderbilt University	1	1					1	1					
Virginia Polytechnic Institute and State University	1		1	1		1							
Wayne State University	2	2		2	2								
Webster University	1	1					1	1					

Table 11 continues...

Academic Institution	All	Men	Women	White	Men	Women	Asian	Men	Women	Black	Men	Women	AI Man
Yale University	1		1				1		1				
Total	92	61	31	55	32	23	32	24	8	5	4	1	
Juris Doctor Degree (n=30) 24 Institutions													
Chicago-Kent College of Law	1		1	1		1							
Columbia University	3	2	1				2	1	1	1	1		
Florida State University	1	1		1	1								
Fordham University	1	1					1	1					
Franklin Pierce Law Center	1	1		1	1								
George Mason University	1		1				1		1				
George Washington University	1	1					1	1					
Georgetown University	1		1				1		1				
Harvard University	4	2	2	3	1	2	1	1					
Loyola Marymount University Law School	1	1		1	1								
Loyola University New Orleans	1	1					1	1					
New England School of Law	1	1		1	1								
New York Law School	1	1		1	1								
New York University	1	1		1	1								
Stanford University	2	2		1	1		1	1					
Touro Law Center	1	1		1	1								
University of California, Los Angeles	1	1		1	1								
University of Chicago	1	1		1	1								
University of Florida	1		1	1		1							
University of Minnesota	1		1				1		1				
University of Pennsylvania	1		1	1		1							
University of the Philippines	1		1				1		1				
University of Southern California	1		1	1		1							

Table 11 continues…

Academic Institution	All	Men	Women	White	Men	Women	Asian	Men	Women	Black	Men	Women	AI Man
Yale University	1	1					1	1					
Total	**30**	**19**	**11**	**17**	**11**	**6**	**12**	**7**	**5**	**1**	**1**		
Doctor of Medicine Degree (n=21) 18 Institutions													
All India Institute of Medical Sciences	1	1					1	1					
Comenius University	1	1		1	1								
Harvard University	4	3	1	2	1	1	2	2					
Johns Hopkins University	1	1		1	1								
Madras Medical College	1	1					1	1					
McGill University	1	1					1	1					
Meharry Medical College	1		1	1		1							
National University of Mexico	1		1	1		1							
New York University	1	1		1	1								
Poznan Medical Academy	1		1	1		1							
University of Algiers	1	1		1	1								
University of California, San Diego	1	1		1	1								
University of Freiburg	1	1		1	1								
University of Göttingen	1	1		1	1								
University of Lyon	1	1		1	1								
University of New Mexico	1		1	1		1							
University of Tübingen	1	1		1	1								
University of Witwatersrand	1	1					1	1					
Total	**21**	**16**	**5**	**15**	**10**	**5**	**6**	**6**					
Doctorate Degree (n=129) 69 Institutions													
American University	1	1								1	1		
Australian National University	2	2		2	2								
Boston University	1		1				1		1				

Table 11 continues…

Academic Institution	All	Men	Women	White	Men	Women	Asian	Men	Women	Black	Men	Women	AI Man
Brandeis University	1	1					1	1					
Columbia University	6	5	1	2	1	1	4	4					
Cornell University	2	2		1	1		1	1					
Czechoslovak Academy of Sciences	1	1		1	1								
Dalhousie University	1	1								1	1		
Drexel University	1	1					1	1					
Harvard University	14	11	3	9	6	3	5	5					
Indian Statistical Institute	1	1					1	1					
Institute of Molecular Biology	1	1		1	1								
Institute of Physical Problems	1	1		1	1								
Julliard School	1		1				1		1				
London School of Economics	1	1		1	1								
Massachusetts Institute of Technology	10	9	1	7	6	1	2	2		1	1		
McGill University	1	1		1	1								
Missouri University of Science and Technology	1	1		1	1								
Moscow Technical University	1	1		1	1								
New School for Social Research	2	2		1	1					1	1		
New York University	1	1		1	1								
Polish Academy of Sciences	1		1	1		1							
Poznan Medical Academy	1		1	1		1							
Princeton University	5	4	1	4	3	1	1	1					
Purdue University	1		1				1		1				
Rensselaer Polytechnic Institute	2	2		2	2								
Rice University	2	2		1	1		1	1					
Stanford University	3	3		2	2		1	1					
State University of New York, Buffalo	1	1		1	1								

Table 11 continues…

Academic Institution	All	Men	Women	White	Men	Women	Asian	Men	Women	Black	Men	Women	AI Man
Tufts University	1	1		1	1								
Ukraine Academy of Sciences	1	1		1	1								
Université de Montréal	1	1		1	1								
University College London	1	1					1	1					
University of Adelaide	1	1		1	1								
University of Alberta	1		1	1		1							
University of Barcelona	1	1		1	1								
University of Belgrade	1		1	1		1							
University of California, Berkeley	8	7	1	5	5		2	1	1	1	1		
University of California, Irvine	1	1					1	1					
University of California, Los Angeles	1		1				1		1				
University of Cambridge	3	1	2	3	1	2							
University of Chicago	5	5		2	2		3	3					
University of Cincinnati	1	1		1	1								
University of Florida	1	1		1	1								
University of Freiburg	1	1		1	1								
University of Göttingen	1	1		1	1								
University of Liverpool	1	1					1	1					
University of London	2	1	1	2	1	1							
University of Miami	2	1	1	2	1	1							
University of Michigan	2	2		1	1		1	1					
University of Milan	1	1		1	1								
University of Naples	1	1		1	1								
University of Oklahoma	1		1	1		1							
University of Oxford	2	1	1	2	1	1							
University of Pennsylvania	4	3	1	3	3		1		1				
University of Rochester	1	1					1	1					
University of Santa Barbara	1	1		1	1								

Table 11 continues…

Academic Institution	All	Men	Women	White	Men	Women	Asian	Men	Women	Black	Men	Women	AI Man
University Southern California	2	2		2	2								
University of Texas, Austin	1	1		1	1								
University of Tokyo	1	1					1	1					
University of Toronto	1	1					1	1					
University of Trieste	1	1		1	1								
University of Utah	1	1		1	1								
University of Waikato	1	1		1	1								
University of Washington	1	1								1	1		
University of Wisconsin, Madison	2	2		2	2								
University of Zurich	1	1		1	1								
Weizmann Institute of Science	1	1		1	1								
Yale University	1	1		1	1								
Total	129	107	22	88	72	16	35	29	6	6	6		

Source: Compiled and computed from June 24, 2015, to January 6, 2016, based on data from: "Great Immigrants: The Pride of America". Carnegie Corporation of New York. http://greatimmigrants.carnegie.org/pride-america/.
Note: AI=American Indian

U.S. State/Country and Geographic Region of Earned Highest/Terminal Higher Education Degrees by Carnegie Corporation of New York's "Pride of America" Honorees, by Race and Sex, 2006-2015

Individual American states, as well as foreign countries and regions, are behind the successes of the higher education institutions located within their jurisdictions. The competiveness of these states, countries, and regions results in public policies that produce competitive institutions. One important reason for this is that many American states, as well as foreign countries and regions, are known worldwide for their higher education institutions or professional sports teams (Kaba, 2011, 2012b, 2013, 2014, 2015, 2016). It is also useful to note that over the past two centuries, there have been different patterns of immigration into the United States' four main regions, without any particular region favored by immigrants during a particular period. (Bankston, III., 2007; Bozorgmehr & Douglas, 2011, p.16; Donato et al., 2007; Greenwood & Ward, 2015; Jaret & Kolozsvari-Wright, 2011; Li & Skop, 2010; Michopoulos, 2013; Scott et al., 2005; Timberlake & Williams, 2012). These immigration patterns have consequences because having talented students and skilled professionals from abroad contributes to a state, country, or region's competitive edge.

Tables 12 and 13 present the American states and regions, as well as the foreign countries and regions, hosting those institutions that conferred the highest or terminal degrees upon the "Pride of America" honorees. According to Table 12, of the 4 associate degrees earned, 3 were from institutions located in Northern America (the United States); 2 in the Northeast: New York (White men), and 1 (White man) in the South (Washington, D.C.). Finally, 1 was earned (Asian woman) from an institution located in Eastern Asia (Hong Kong).

For bachelor's degrees, 59 (77.6%) of the total 76 were earned at institutions in Northern America: 56 in the United States (39 by men and 17 by women), and 3 in Canada (all women). Of the 56 degrees earned in the United States, 25 (44.6%) were from institutions in the Northeast (18 men and 7 women) with New York accounting for 14 (9 by men and 5 by women), Massachusetts for 3 (all men), and Pennsylvania for 3 (2 by men and 1 woman). 14 (25%) degrees were earned in the South (9 by men and 5 by women), with Florida accounting for 5 (3 by men and 2 by women) and Texas for 4 (2 by men and 2 by women); 12 (21.4%) degrees were earned from institutions in the West (8 by men and 4 by women), with 10 of them from California (6 by men and 4 by women); and 5 (8.9%) from the Midwest (4 by men and 1 woman), with 2 (all men) from Illinois. Two bachelor's degrees earned in Southern Africa: both in South Africa (1 man and 1 woman). Two bachelor's degrees earned in Asia: 1 in South Korea, Eastern Asia (1 man), and 1 in Pakistan, Southern Asia (1 woman). Twelve bachelor's degrees were earned in Europe (10 by men and 2 by women): 10 (83.3%) in Northern Europe, including 7 in the United Kingdom (all men), and 2 in Ireland (all men). Finally, 1 bachelor's degree was earned in Australia, Oceania (1 woman).

For a racial breakdown, Whites earned 52 bachelor's degrees (35 by men and 17 by women), with 37 (71.2%) of them earned in Northern America (24 by men and 13 women); 34 in the United States (21 by men and 13 by women) and 3 in Canada (all men). Of the 34 bachelor's degrees earned in the United States, 15 (44.1%) of them were earned in the Northeast (11 by men and 4 by women), with 8 earned in New York (5 by men and 3 by women), and 3 in Pennsylvania (2 by men and 1 woman): 8 (23.5%) in the South (4 by men and 4 by women), with Florida accounting for 4 (2 by men and 2 by women); 8 (23.5%) in the West (4 by men and 4 by women), with California accounting for 7 (4 by women and 3 by men); and 3 (8.8%) in the Midwest (2 by men and 1 woman), with Illinois and Wisconsin accounting for 1 each (both men), and Minnesota accounting for 1 (a woman). Whites earned 2 bachelor's degrees in South Africa, Africa (1 man and 1 woman) and 12 bachelor's degrees in Europe (10 by men and 2 by women), with 10 (83.3%) in Northern Europe (all men): 7 in the United Kingdom, 2 in Ireland, and 1 in Norway; and 1 each in Poland, Eastern Europe (a woman), and France, Western Europe (a woman). Finally, one white woman earned a bachelor's degree in Oceania (Australia). Asians earned 14 bachelor's degrees (10 by men and 4 by women), with 12 (85.7%) in Northern America, all in the United States (9 by men and 3 by women): 8 (66.7%) in the Northeast (5 by men and 3 by women), with New York accounting for 4 (2 by men and 2 by women) and Massachusetts for 2 (both men); 2 (16.7%) in the South (all men), with 1 each in Florida and Texas; and 1 (8.3%) each in the Midwest (Illinois) and the West (California). Asians earned 2 bachelor's degrees Asia (1 man in South

Korea and 1 woman in Pakistan). Nine Blacks earned bachelor's degrees (8 men and 1 woman), all in the United States. Of these 9 bachelor's degrees, 4 (44.4%) were earned in the South (3 men and 1 woman), with 2 (both men) earned in Washington, D.C., 1 each in Alabama (1 man) and Texas (1 woman); 2 (22.2%) in the Northeast (all men in New York); 2 (22.2%) in the West (all men in Arizona and California); and 1 (11.1%) in the Midwest (1 man in Ohio). Finally, 1 American Indian man earned a bachelor's degree in California. Of the 92 master's degrees (60 by men and 32 by women), 87 (94.6%) were earned in Northern America, with the United States accounting for 86 (58 by men and 28 by women) and Canada for 1 (1 woman). Of the 86 master's degrees earned in the United States, 39 (45.3%) were earned in the Northeast (27 by men and 12 by women), with New York accounting for 18 (13 by men and 5 by women), Massachusetts for 9 (7 by men and 2 by women), and Pennsylvania for 5 (3 by women and 2 by men); 18 (20.9%) in the West (12 by men and 6 by women), with California accounting for 16 (10 by men and 6 by women); 16 (18.6%) in the South (9 by men and 7 by women), with Maryland accounting for 4 (3 by women and 1 man), Washington, D.C., for 3 (2 by women and 1 man), and 2 each in Florida (all by men), Texas, and Virginia (each 1 man and 1 woman); and 13 (15.1%) in the Midwest (10 by men and 3 by women), with Illinois accounting for 7 (5 by men and 2 by women), and Michigan accounting for 3 (all men). Five master's degrees earned in Europe (3 by women and 2 by men); 3 in Northern Europe (all in the United Kingdom) (2 by women and 1 man), 1 in Russia, Eastern Europe (1 man), and 1 in Switzerland, Western Europe (1 woman).

For a racial breakdown, Whites earned 55 master's degrees (32 men and 23 women), 51 (92.7%) in Northern America (30 by men and 21 by women): 50 in the United States (30 by men and 20 by women), and 1 degree in Canada (1 woman). Of the 50 master's degrees earned in the United States by Whites, 20 (40%) were earned in the Northeast (13 by men and 7 by women), with 10 in New York (6 by men and 4 by women), 4 each in Massachusetts (all men) and Pennsylvania (2 by men and 2 by women); 12 (24%) in the South (6 by men and 6 by women), with Maryland accounting for 3 (all women), and Washington, D.C., accounting for 3 (2 by women and 1 man); 11 (225%) in the West, all in California (6 by women and 5 by men); and 7 (14%) in the Midwest (6 by men and 1 woman), with 3 each (all men) in Illinois and Michigan, and 1 in Minnesota (a woman). Whites earned 4 master's degrees Europe (2 by men and 2 by women), with 2 (1 man and 1 woman) in the United Kingdom, Northern Europe, and 1 each in Russia, Eastern Europe, and Switzerland, Western Europe (both men). Asians earned 32 master's degrees (24 men and 8 women), with 31 (96.9%) in the United States (24 by men and 7 by women) and 1 in Europe (a woman in the United Kingdom). Of the 31 master's degrees earned in the United States by Asians, 16 (51.6%) we earned in the Northeast (12 by men and 4 by women), with New York accounting for 6 (5 by men and 1 woman) and Massachusetts for 5 (3 by women and 2 by men); 7 (22.6%) in the West (all men), with California accounting for 5; 5 (16.1%) in the Midwest (3 by men and 2 by women), with Illinois accounting for 3 (2 by women and 1 man); and 3 (9.7%) in the South (2 by men and 1 woman), with 1 each in Maryland and Tennessee (1 man each), and Texas (a woman). Finally, Blacks earned 5 master's degrees (4 by men and 1 woman), all in the United States: 3 (60%) in the Northeast (2 by men and 1 woman), with New York accounting for 2 (all men) and Rhode Island for 1 (a woman); and 1 (20%) male each in the Midwest (Illinois) and the South (Virginia).

As regards the Juris Doctor degrees, 29 were earned in the United States and 1 by a woman in the Philippines, Southeastern Asia. Of the 29 degrees earned in the United States, 15 (51.7%) were earned in the Northeast (11 men and 4 women), with New York accounting for 7 (6 men and 1 woman), and Massachusetts accounting for 5 (3 men and 2 women); 6 (20.7%) in the South (3 men and 3 women), with Florida and Washington, D.C., each accounting for 2 (1 man and 1 woman each); 5 (17.2%) in the West, with California accounting for all of them (4 men and 1 woman); and 3 (10.3%) in the Midwest (2 women and 1 man), with Illinois accounting for 2 (1 man and 1 woman) and Minnesota for 1 (a woman). For a racial breakdown, Whites earned 17 Juris Doctor degrees (11 men and 6 women), all in the United States: 9 (52.9%) in the Northeast (6 men and 3 women), with 4 in Massachusetts (2 men and 2 women) and 3 in New York (all men); 4 (23.5%) in the West, all in California (3 men and 1 woman); and 2 (11.8%) each in the Midwest, all in Illinois (1 man and 1 woman), and the South (1 man and 1 woman). Asians earned 12 Juris Doctor degrees (7 men and 5 women), with 11 in the United States (7 men and 4 women) and 1 (a woman) in the Philippines, Southeastern Asia. Of the

11 Juris Doctor degrees earned in the United States, 5 (45.5%) were earned in the Northeast (4 men and 1 woman), with New York accounting for 3 (2 men and 1 woman); and 1 (9.1%) each in the Midwest (Minnesota, a woman), and the West (California, a man). Finally, there is 1 Black man who earned a Juris Doctor degree in New York, Northeast United States.

Of the 21 doctor of medicine degrees earned by 21 honorees (16 men and 5 women), 10 (47.6%) were earned in Northern America (7 men and 3 women): 9 earned in the United States (6 men and 3 women) and 1 in Canada (a man). Of the 9 doctor of medicine degrees earned in the United States, 5 (55.5%) were earned in the Northeast (4 men and 1 woman), with Massachusetts accounting for 4 (3 men and 1 woman) and New York for 1 (a man); 2 (22.2%) each in the South, Maryland (a man) and Tennessee (a woman), and in the West, California (a man), and New Mexico (a woman). One woman earned a doctor of medicine degree in Mexico, Central America (a woman). Two women earned their degrees in India, Southern Asia. Six doctor of medicine degrees were earned in Europe: 4 in Western Europe, with Germany accounting for 3 (all men) and France for 1; and 2 in Eastern Europe, with one each in the Czech Republic (a man) and Poland (a woman). For a racial breakdown, of the 21 doctor of medicine degrees earned (16 men and 5 women), Whites earned 15 (71.4%) (10 men and 5 women): 7 (46.7%) in the United States (4 men and 3 women), 6 (40%) in Europe, and 1 (6.7%) each in Algeria, Northern Africa (a man), and Mexico, Central America (a woman). Of the 7 doctor of medicine degrees earned in the United States, 3 (42.9%) were earned in the Northeast (2 men and 1 woman), with Massachusetts accounting for 2 (1 man and 1 woman) and New York for 1 (a man). Of the 6 doctor of medicine degrees earned in Europe, 4 (66.7%) were earned in Western Europe (all men), with Germany accounting for 3 and France for 1; and 2 (33.3%) in Eastern Europe, with the Czech Republic accounting for 1 man and Poland for 1 woman. Finally, Asians earned 6 doctor of medicine degrees: 3 (50%) in Northern America (all men), with 2 in the Northeast United States (Massachusetts) and 1 in Canada; 2 (33.3%) in India, Southern Asia; and 1 (16.7%) in South Africa, Southern Africa.

Of the 129 doctorate degrees earned (107 men and 22 women), 97 (75.2%) were earned from institutions located in Northern America (82 by men and 15 by women), with 92 degrees earned in the United States (78 by men and 14 by women), and 5 degrees earned in Canada (4 by men and 1 woman). Of the 92 doctorate degrees earned in the United States, 54 (58.7%) were from institutions in the Northeast (45 by men and 9 by women), with Massachusetts accounting for 27 (22 by men and 5 by women), New York for 16 (14 by men and 2 by women), and New Jersey and Pennsylvania each for 5 (4 by men and 1 woman each); 18 (19.6%) in the West (16 men and 2 women), with California accounting for 16 (14 men and 2 women); 12 (13%) in the Midwest (11 by men and 1 woman), with Illinois accounting for 5 (all men), and 2 each in Michigan and Wisconsin (all men each); and 8 (8.7%) in the South (6 by men and 2 by women), with Florida accounting for 3 (2 by men and 1 woman) and Texas for 3 (all men). Three degrees were earned in Asia (all men): Japan (Eastern Asia), India (Southern Asia), and Israel (Western Asia). Twenty-five degrees were earned in Europe (18 men and 7 women), with 10 in Northern Europe (6 by men and 4 by women), all in the United Kingdom; 7 in Eastern Europe (5 by men and 2 by women), with Russia accounting for 3 (all men) and Poland for 2 (both women); 5 (4 by men and 1 woman) in Southern Europe, with Italy accounting for 3 (all men); and 3 (all men) in Western Europe, with Germany accounting for 2 (all men). Finally, 4 doctorate degrees were earned in Oceania (all men), with Australia accounting for 3 and New Zealand for 1.

For a racial breakdown, Whites earned 88 doctorate degrees (72 by men and 16 by women), with Northern America accounting for 60 degrees (69%) (51 by men and 9 by women): 57 (95%) in the United States (49 by men and 8 by women) and 3 (5%) in Canada (2 by men and 1 woman). Of the 57 doctorate degrees earned by Whites in the United States, 33 (57.9%) were earned in the Northeast (27 by men and 6 by women), with Massachusetts accounting for 17 (13 men and 4 women), New York for 8 (7 men and 1 woman), and New Jersey for 4 (3 men and 1 woman); 11 (19.2%) in the West (all men), with California accounting for 10; 7 (12.3%) in the Midwest (all men), with Illinois and Wisconsin each accounting for 2; and 6 (10.5%) in the South (4 men and 2 women). One White man earned a degree in Israel, Western Asia. Whites earned 22 doctorate degrees in Europe (16 men and 6 women): 8 in Northern Europe, all in the United Kingdom (4 by men and 4 by women); 7 in Eastern Europe (5 by men and 2 by women), with 3 in

Russia (all men) and 2 in Poland (all women); 5 in Southern Europe (4 men and 1 woman), with Italy accounting for 3 (all men); and 3 in Western Europe (all men), with Germany accounting for two. White men earned all 4 doctorate degrees in Oceania, with Australia accounting for three.

Asians earned 35 doctorate degrees (29 by men and 6 by women): 31 (88.6%) in Northern America (25 men and 6 women), with 30 degrees earned in the United States and 1 in Canada. Of the 30 degrees earned in the United States by Asians (24 by men and 6 by women), 19 (63.3%) were earned in the Northeast (16 by men and 3 by women), with Massachusetts accounting for 9 (8 men and 1 women) and New York for 7 (6 men and 1 woman); 5 (15.6%) in the Midwest (4 men and 1 woman), with 3 earned in Illinois: 5 (15.6%) in the West, all in California (3 men and 2 women); and 1 man (3%) in the South (Texas). Two Asian men earned 2 doctorate degrees in Asia (Japan and India). Two Asian men earned a doctorate degree each in Europe (both in the United Kingdom). Finally, 6 Black men earned 6 doctorate degrees in Northern America, with 5 in the United States and 1 in Canada. Of the 5 doctorate degrees earned in the United States, 2 (40%) each were earned in the Northeast and West, and 1 (20%) in the South (Table 12).

Table 12. U.S. State/Country of Earned Highest/Terminal Higher Education Degrees of Carnegie Corporation of New York's "Pride of America" Honorees, by Race and Sex, 2006-2015

Academic Degree	All	Men	Women	White Men	Women	Asian Men	Women	Black Men	Women	AI Men
Region/Country	#	#	#	#	#	#	#	#	#	#
Associate/Diploma (n=4)	4	3	1	4	3		1				
Northern America	3	2		3	3						
United States	3	3		3	3						
Northeast	2	2		2	2						
New York	2	2		2	2						
South	1	1		1	1						

Table 12 continues...

Academic Degree	All	Men	Women	White	Men	Women	Asian	Men	Women	Black	Men	Women	AI Men
Washington, D.C.	1	1		1	1								
Asia	1		1				1		1				
Eastern Asia	1		1				1		1				
Hong Kong, China	1		1				1		1				
Bachelor's Degree (n=76)	76	54	22	52	35	17	14	10	4	9	8	1	
Northern America	59	42	17	37	24	13	12	9	3	9	8	1	
Canada	3	3		3	3								
United States	56	39	17	34	21	13	12	9	3	9	8	1	
Midwest	5	4	1	3	2	1	1	1		1	1		
Illinois	2	2		1	1		1	1					
Minnesota	1		1	1		1							
Ohio	1	1								1	1		
Wisconsin	1	1		1	1								
Northeast	25	18	7	15	11	4	8	5	3	2	2		
Connecticut	2	2		2	2								
Massachusetts	3	3		1	1		2	2					
New Jersey	1		1				1		1				
New York	14	9	5	8	5	3	4	2	2	2	2		
Pennsylvania	3	2	1	3	2	1							
Rhode Island	1	1					1	1					
Vermont	1	1		1	1								
South	14	9	5	8	4	4	2	2		4	3	1	
Alabama	1	1								1	1		
Florida	5	3	2	4	2	2	1	1					
Kentucky	1		1	1		1							
Maryland	1	1		1	1								
Texas	4	2	2	2	1	1	1	1		1		1	

Table 12 continues…

Academic Degree	All	Men	Women	White	Men	Women	Asian	Men	Women	Black	Men	Women	AI Men
Washington, D.C.	2	2								2	2		
West	12	8	4	8	4	4	1	1		2	2		1
Arizona	1	1								1	1		
California	10	6	4	7	3	4	1	1		1	1		1
Washington	1	1		1	1								
Africa	2	1	1	2	1	1							
Southern Africa	2	1	1	2	1	1							
South Africa	2	1	1	2	1	1							
Asia	2	1	1				2	1	1				
Eastern Asia	1	1					1	1					
South Korea	1	1					1	1					
Southern Asia	1		1				1		1				
Pakistan	1		1				1		1				
Europe	12	10	2	12	10	2							
Eastern Europe	1		1	1		1							
Poland	1		1	1		1							
Northern Europe	10	10		10	10								
Ireland	2	2		2	2								
Norway	1	1		1	1								
United Kingdom	7	7		7	7								
Western Europe	1		1	1		1							
France	1		1	1		1							

92

Table 12 continues...

Academic Degree	All	Men	Women	White	Men	Women	Asian	Men	Women	Black	Men	Women	AI Men
Oceania	1		1	1		1							
Australia	1		1	1		1							
Master's Degree (n=92)	92	60	32	55	32	23	32	24	8	5	4	1	
Northern America	87	58	29	51	30	21	31	24	7	5	4	1	
Canada	1		1	1		1							
United States	86	58	28	50	30	20	31	24	7	5	4	1	
Midwest	13	10	3	7	6	1	5	3	2	1	1		
Illinois	7	5	2	3	3		3	1	2	1	1		
Michigan	3	3		3	3								
Minnesota	1		1	1		1							
Missouri	1	1					1	1					
Wisconsin	1	1					1	1					
Northeast	39	27	12	20	13	7	16	12	4	3	2	1	
Connecticut	1		1				1		1				
Massachusetts	9	7	2	4	4		5	3	2				
New Hampshire	1	1					1	1					
New York	18	13	5	10	6	4	6	5	1	2	2		
Pennsylvania	5	3	2	4	2	2	1	1					
Rhode Island	3	2	1				2	2		1		1	
Vermont	2	1	1	2	1	1							
South	16	9	7	12	6	6	3	2	1	1	1		
Florida	2	2		2	2								
Georgia	1	1		1	1								
Maryland	4	1	3	3		3	1	1					
North Carolina	1	1		1	1								
Tennessee	1	1					1	1					
Texas	2	1	1	1	1		1		1				
Virginia	2	1	1	1		1				1	1		

Table 12 continues...

Academic Degree	All	Men	Women	White	Men	Women	Asian	Men	Women	Black	Men	Women	AI Men
Washington, D.C.	3	1	2	3	1	2							
West	18	12	6	11	5	6	7	7					
California	16	10	6	11	5	6	5	5					
Colorado	1	1					1	1					
Oregon	1	1					1	1					
Europe	5	2	3	4	2	2	1		1				
Eastern Europe	1	1		1	1								
Russia	1	1		1	1								
Northern Europe	3	1	2	2	1	1	1		1				
United Kingdom	3	1	2	2	1	1	1		1				
Western Europe	1		1	1		1							
Switzerland	1		1	1		1							
Juris Doctor Degree (n=30)	30	19	11	17	11	6	12	7	5	1	1		
Northern America	29	19	10	17	11	6	11	7	4	1	1		
United States	29	19	10	17	11	6	11	7	4	1	1		
Midwest	3	1	2	2	1	1	1		1				
Illinois	2	1	1	2	1	1							
Minnesota	1		1				1		1				
Northeast	15	11	4	9	6	3	5	4	1	1	1		
Connecticut	1	1					1	1					
Massachusetts	5	3	2	4	2	2	1	1					
New Hampshire	1	1		1	1								
New York	7	6	1	3	3		3	2	1	1	1		
Pennsylvania	1		1	1		1							
South	6	3	3	2	1	1	4	2	2				
Florida	2	1	1	2	1	1							

Table 12 continues…

Academic Degree	All	Men	Women	White	Men	Women	Asian	Men	Women	Black	Men	Women	AI Men
Louisiana	1	1					1	1					
Virginia	1		1				1		1				
Washington, D.C.	2	1	1				2	1	1				
West	5	4	1	4	3	1	1	1					
California	5	4	1	4	3	1	1	1					
Asia	1		1				1		1				
Southeastern Asia	1		1				1		1				
Philippines	1		1				1		1				
Doctor of Medicine Degree (21)	21	16	5	15	10	5	6	6					
Northern America	10	7	3	7	4	3	3	3					
Canada	1	1					1	1					
United States	9	6	3	7	4	3	2	2					
Midwest													
Northeast	5	4	1	3	2	1	2	2					
Massachusetts	4	3	1	2	1	1	2	2					
New York	1	1		1	1								
South	2	1	1	2	1	1							
Maryland	1	1		1	1								
Tennessee	1		1	1		1							
West	2	1	1	2	1	1							
California	1	1		1	1								
New Mexico	1		1	1		1							
Africa	2	2		1	1		1	1					
Northern Africa	1	1		1	1								
Algeria	1	1		1	1								

Table 12 continues…

Academic Degree	All	Men	Women	White	Men	Women	Asian	Men	Women	Black	Men	Women	AI Men
Southern Africa	1	1					1	1					
South Africa	1	1					1	1					
Latin America & the Caribbean	1		1	1		1							
Central America	1		1	1		1							
Mexico	1		1	1		1							
Asia	2	2					2	2					
Southern Asia	2	2					2	2					
India	2	2					2	2					
Europe	6	5	1	6	5	1							
Eastern Europe	2	1	1	2	1	1							
Czech Republic	1	1		1	1								
Poland	1		1	1		1							
Western Europe	4	4		4	4								
France	1	1		1	1								
Germany	3	3		3	3								
Doctorate Degree (n=129)	**129**	**107**	**22**	**88**	**72**	**16**	**35**	**29**	**6**	**6**	**6**		
Northern America	97	82	15	60	51	9	31	25	6	6	6		
Canada	5	4	1	3	2	1	1	1		1	1		
United States	92	78	14	57	49	8	30	24	6	5	5		
Midwest	12	11	1	7	7		5	4	1				
Illinois	5	5		2	2		3	3					
Indiana	1		1				1		1				
Michigan	2	2		1	1		1	1					
Missouri	1	1		1	1								
Ohio	1	1		1	1								
Wisconsin	2	2		2	2								
Northeast	54	45	9	33	27	6	19	16	3	2	2		

Table 12 continues...

Academic Degree	All	Men	Women	White	Men	Women	Asian	Men	Women	Black	Men	Women	AI Men
Connecticut	1	1		1	1								
Massachusetts	27	22	5	17	13	4	9	8	1	1	1		
New Jersey	5	4	1	4	3	1	1	1					
New York	16	14	2	8	7	1	7	6	1	1	1		
Pennsylvania	5	4	1	3	3		2	1	1				
South	8	6	2	6	4	2	1	1		1	1		
Florida	3	2	1	3	2	1							
Oklahoma	1		1	1		1							
Texas	3	3		2	2		1	1					
Washington, D.C.	1	1								1	1		
West	18	16	2	11	11		5	3	2	2	2		
California	16	14	2	10	10		5	3	2	1	1		
Utah	1	1		1	1								
Washington	1	1								1	1		
Asia	3	3		1	1		2	2					
Eastern Asia	1	1					1	1					
Japan	1	1					1	1					
Southern Asia	1	1					1	1					
India	1	1					1	1					
Western Asia	1	1		1	1								
Israel	1	1		1	1								
Europe	25	18	7	23	16	7	2	2					
Eastern Europe	7	5	2	7	5	2							
Czech Republic	1	1		1	1								
Poland	2		2	2		2							
Russia	3	3		3	3								
Ukraine	1	1		1	1								

Table 12 continues...

Academic Degree	All	Men	Women	White	Men	Women	Asian	Men	Women	Black	Men	Women	AI Men
Northern Europe	10	6	4	8	4	4	2	2					
United Kingdom	10	6	4	8	4	4	2	2					
Southern Europe	5	4	1	5	4	1							
Italy	3	3		3	3								
Serbia	1		1	1		1							
Spain	1	1		1	1								
Western Europe	3	3		3	3								
Germany	2	2		2	2								
Switzerland	1	1		1	1								
Oceania	4	4		4	4								
Australia	3	3		3	3								
New Zealand	1	1		1	1								

Source: Compiled and computed from June 24, 2015, to January 6, 2016, based on data from: "Great Immigrants: The Pride of America". Carnegie Corporation of New York. http://greatimmigrants.carnegie.org/pride-america/; The United Nations classifications of regions can be found at: "Composition of macro geographical (continental) regions, geographical sub-regions, and selected economic and other groupings," United Nations Statistics Division, Department of Economic and Social Affairs. Retrieved on May 19, 2016: http://unstats.un.org/unsd/methods/m49/m49regin.htm.

Note: AI=American Indian

Table 13 below groups all earned degrees according to the holder's region and sex. Of the 352 combined higher education degrees earned by the 323 "Pride of America" honorees, 259 (73.6%) were earned by men and 93 (26.4%) by women. Of the 352 combined degrees, 285 (81%) were earned in Northern America (211 by men and 60 by women), with the United States accounting for 275 (78.1% of the total) and Canada for 10 (2.8% of total); 48 (13.6%) in Europe; 9 (2.6%) in Asia; 5 (1.4%) in Oceania (4 men and 1 woman); 4 (1.1%) in Africa (3 by men and 1 woman); and 1 (0.3% of total) in Central America (1 woman). Of the 275 degrees earned in the United States (203 men and 72 women), 140 (50.9%, but 39.8% of total) were earned in the Northeast (107 men and 33 women); 55 (20%, but 15.6% of total) in the West (41 by men and 14 by women); 47 (17.1%, but 13.3% of total) in the South (29 by men and 18 by women); and 33 (12%, but 9.4% of total) in the Midwest (26 by men and 7 by women). Of the 10 degrees earned in Canada, 8 (80%, but 2.8% of total) are men, and 2 (20%, but 0.6% of total) are women. Of the 48 degrees earned in Europe (35 by men and 13 by women) 23 (47.9%, but 6.5% of total) were earned in Northern Europe (17 by men and 6 by women); 12 (25%, but 3.4% of total) in Eastern Europe (7 by men and 5 by women); 9 (18.8%, but 2.6% of total) in Western Europe (7 by men and 2 by women); and 4 (8.3%, but 1.1% of total) in Southern Europe (all men). Of the 9 degrees earned in Asia, 4 (44.4%, but 1.1% of total) were earned in Southern Asia (3 by men and 1 woman); 3 (33.3%, but 0.9% of total) in eastern Asia (2 by men and 1 woman); and 1 (11.1%, but 0.3% of total) each Southeastern Asia and Western Asia (Table 13).

Table 13. World Region where Academic Degrees were earned by Carnegie Corporation of New York's "Pride of America" Honorees, by Sex, 2006-2015
N=352 degrees

All								
Academic Degree Region/Country	All #	% of Total	Men #	% of Total	% of Men	Women #	% of Total	% of Women
Northern America	285	81	211	60	23.2	74	21	79.6
Canada	10	2.8	8	2	3.1	2	0.6	2.2
United States	275	78.1	203	57.7	78.4	72	20.5	77.4
Midwest	33	9.4	26	7.4	10	7	2	7.5

Table 13 continues…

All Academic Degree Region/Country	All #	% of Total	Men #	% of Total	% of Men	Women #	% of Total	% of Women
Northeast	140	39.8	107	30.4	41.3	33	9.4	35.5
South	47	13.3	29	8.2	11.2	18	5.1	19.4
West	55	15.6	41	11.6	15.9	14	4	4.3
Africa	4	1.1	3	0.9	1.2	1	0.3	1.1
Northern Africa	1	0.3	1	0.3	0.4			
Southern Africa	3	0.9	2	0.6	0.8	1	0.3	1.1
Latin America & the Caribbean	1	0.3				1	0.3	1.1
Central America	1	0.3				1	0.3	1.1
Asia	9	2.6	6	1.7	2.3	3	0.9	3.2
Eastern Asia	3	0.9	2	0.6	0.8	1	0.3	1.1
Southern Asia	4	1.1	3	0.9	1.2	1	0.3	1.1
Southeastern Asia	1	0.3				1	0.3	1.1
Western Asia	1	0.3	1	0.3	0.4			
Europe	48	13.6	35	9.9	13.5	13	3.7	13.8
Eastern Europe	12	3.4	7	2	2.7	5	1.4	5.4
Northern Europe	23	6.5	17	4.8	6.6	6	1.7	6.5
Southern Europe	4	1.1	4	1.1	1.5			
Western Europe	9	2.6	7	2	2.7	2	0.6	2.2
Oceania	5	1.4	4	1.1	1.5	1	0.3	1.1
Overall Total	352		259	73.6		93	26.4	

Source: Compiled and computed from June 24, 2015, to January 6, 2016, based on data from: "Great Immigrants: The Pride of America". Carnegie Corporation of New York. http://greatimmigrants.carnegie.or g/pride-america/; The United Nations classifications of regions can be found at: "Composition of macro geographical (continental) regions, geographical sub-regions, and selected economic and other groupings," United Nations Statistics Division, Department of Economic and Social Affairs. Retrieved on May 19, 2016: http://unstats.un.org/unsd/ methods/m49/m49regin.htm.

Net Worth of a Selected Number of "Pride of America" Honorees (n=122)

Table 14 presents available data on the net worth of 122 (30%) of the 408 "Pride of America" honorees. The educational attainment data presented above support the claim that there is a correlation or association between level of education and wealth accumulation in the United States. This is especially the case for those with earned college degrees in the United States and categorized as White or Asian. These honorees are among the country's wealthiest individuals both in this country and the world (Allen, 2006; Bideshi & Kposowa, 2012; Chilea & Kassai, 2016; Cobb-Clark & Hildebrand, 2006; Guo, 2015; Kaushal, 2011; Petras, 2008; Wai, 2015; Wai & Rindermann, 2015).

Of these 122 honorees, men comprise 87 (71.3%), and women 35 (28.7%). Their total net worth is $113.4 billion, with men accounting for $106.9 billion (94.3%), and women for $6.51 billion (5.7%). For a racial breakdown, Whites account for 83 (68%), with 56 men and 27 women; Asians, 27 (22.1%), with 21 men and 6 women; and Blacks 12 (9.8%), with 10 men and 2 women. The 83 Whites have a net worth of $93.3 billion (82.3% of total), with men accounting for $88.1 billion (94.4%, but 77.7% of total, and 82.4% of total for all men), and women for $5.23 billion (5.6%, but 4.6% of total, and 80.4% of the total for all women). They are from 31 nations, with the following ones having 5 or more: Canada, 12 (11 men and 1 woman); England, UK, 7 (4 men and 3 women); Germany, 7 (6 men and 1 woman); and the Czech Republic and Mexico each, 5 (3 women and 2 men each). For the 27 Asians, their net worth is $19.5 billion (17.1% of total), with men accounting for $18.23 billion (93.6%, but 16.1% of total, and 17.1% of the total of all men) and women for $1.25 billion (6.4%, but 1.1% of total, and 19.2% of total of all women). They are from 9 nations, with 3 or more from each of the following: India, 10 (9 men and 1 woman); Taiwan, 4 (3 men and 1 woman); China, 3 (2 men and 1 woman); Japan, 3 (2 women and 1 man); and South Korea, 3 (all men). For the 12 Blacks, their net worth is $647.5 million (0.7% of total), with men accounting for $616 million (95.1%, but 0.7% to total, and 0.6% of total of all men), and women for $31.5 million (4.86%, but 0.03% of total, and 0.49% of total of all women). They are from 9 nations, with 3 from the Dominican

Republic (all men) and 2 from Jamaica (1 man and 1 woman) (Table 14).

Table 14. Net Worth of Carnegie Corporation of New York's "Pride of America" Honorees, by Sex and Race, 2006-2015 (as of mid-November 2015 and before)
n=122

Race/Previous Nationality Race	Number Both Sexes	% of Total	% of Men	% of Total	% of Men	% of Women	% of Total	% of Women	Net Worth Both Sexes U.S. $	% of Total	Men	% of Total	% of Men	Women	% of Total	% of Women
Asian																
China	3	11.1	2	7.4	9.5	1	3.7	16.7	1,623,000,009	8.3	1,620,000,000	8.3	8.9	3,000,000	0.015	0.2
France	1	3.7	1	3.7	4.8	..			20,000,000	0.1	20,000,000	0.1	0.1	..	..	
India	10	37.0	9	33.3	42.9	1	3.7	16.7	2,162,500,011	11.1	2,031,500,000	10.4	11.1	131,000,000	0.67	10.
Japan	3	11.1	1	3.7	4.8	2	7.4	33.3	507,553,523	2.6	5,000,000	0.026	0.27	502,553,523	2.6	40.
Philippines	1	3.7	..	..	..	1	3.7	16.7	600,000,000	3.1	..	..	..	600,000,000	3.1	48.
South Africa	1	3.7	1	3.7	4.8	..	..	..	12,400,000,000	63.7	12,400,000,000	63.7	68.0	..	..	..
South Korea	3	11.1	3	11.1	14.3	..	..	..	27,000,000	0.1	27,000,000	0.14	0.1	..	..	..
Taiwan	4	14.8	3	11.1	14.3	1	3.7	16.7	2,133,400,012	11.0	2,122,000,000	10.9	11.6	11,400,000	0.058	0.9
Vietnam	1	3.7	1	3.7	4.8	..	..	..	827,512	0.004	827,512	0.005	0.005	..	..	..
Total	27	100.0	21	77.8	100	6	22.2	100	19,474,281,067	100.0	18,226,327,512	93.6	100.0	1,247,953,52	6.4	100
% of Overall Total		22.1		17.2	24.1		4.9	17.1		17.1		16.1	17.1		1.1	19.
Black																
Benin	1	8.3	1	8.3	10	..	..	..	12,000,000	1.9	12,000,000	1.9	1.9	..	..	..
Dem. Rep. of Congo	1	8.3	1	8.3	10	..	..	..	75,000,000	11.6	75,000,000	11.6	12.2	..	..	..
Dominican Republic	3	25.0	3	25.0	30	..	..	..	205,000,000	31.7	205,000,000	31.7	33.3	..	..	..
England, UK	1	8.3	1	8.3	10	..	..	..	7,000,000	1.1	7,000,000	1.1	1.1	..	..	..
Ghana	1	8.3	1	8.3	10	..	..	..	12,000,000	1.9	12,000,000	1.9	1.9	..	..	..
Jamaica	2	16.7	1	16.7	10	1	8.3	50	86,500,014	13.4	85,000,000	13.1	13.8	1,500,000	0.23	4.8
Nigeria	1	8.3	1	8.3	10	..	..	..	200,000,000	30.9	200,000,000	30.9	32.5	..	..	
Saint Vincent and the Grenadines	1	8.3	1	8.3	10	..		..	20,000,000	3.1	20,000,000	3.1	3.2	..	..	..
Somalia	1	8.3	..	..	..	1	8.3	50	30,000,000	4.6	..	..	..	30,000,000	4.63	95
Total	12	100.0	10	91.7	100	2	16.7	100	647,500,014	100.0	616,000,000	95.1	100.0	31,500,000	4.86	10
% of Overall Total		9.8		8.2	11.5		1.6	5.7		0.7		0.7	0.6		0.03	0.
White																
Afghanistan	1	1.2	1	1.2	1.8	..			5,000,000	0.005	5,000,000	0.005	0.006	..	..	..
Australia	2	2.4	1	1.2	1.8	1	1.2	3.7	12,603,000,014	13.51	12,600,000,000	13.5	14.31	3,000,000	0.0032	0.
Austria	1	1.2	1	1.2	1.8	..			300,000,000	0.32	300,000,000	0.32	0.34	..	..	..

Table 14 continues…

Race/Previous Nationality	Number	% of Total	% of Men	% of Total	% of Men	Women	% of Total	% of Women	Net Worth Both Sexes U.S. $	% of Total	Men	% of Total	% of Men	Women	% of Total	% of Women
Race Asian	Both Sexes															
Canada	12	14.5	11	13.3	19.6	1	1.2	3.7	5,870,000,004	6.29	3,520,000,000	3.8	4.00	2,350,000,000	2.5	44.95
Colombia	2	2.4	1	1.2	1.8	1	1.2	3.7	125,000,000	0.13	25,000,000	0.027	0.03	100,000,000	0.11	1.91
Croatia	1	1.2		0.0	0.0	1	1.2	3.7	3,750,000	0.00	..	..		3,750,000	4	0.07
Cuba	4	4.8	2	2.4	3.6	2	2.4	7.4	553,726,517	0.59	52,769,013	0.057	0.06	500,957,504	0.54	9.58
Czech Republic	5	6.0	2	2.4	3.6	3	3.6	11.1	95,000,000	0.10	60,000,000	0.064	0.07	35,000,000	0.038	0.67
Dominican Republic	1	1.2	1	1.2	1.8	..			200,000,000	0.21	200,000,000	0.21	0.23	..	..	..
Egypt	1	1.2	1	1.2	1.8	..			1,690,000,000	1.81	1,690,000,000	1.8	1.92	..	..	..
England, UK	7	8.4	4	4.8	7.1	3	3.6	11.1	287,000,000	0.31	67,000,000	0.072	0.08	220,000,000	0.24	4.21
France	1	1.2	1	1.2	1.8	..			8,000,000,000	8.58	8,000,000,000	8.6	9.09	..	..	..
Germany	7	8.4	6	7.2	10.7	1	1.2	3.7	7,906,000,009	8.48	7,836,000,000	8.4	8.90	70,000,000	0.75	1.34
Greece	1	1.2		0.0	0.0	1	1.2	3.7	50,000,000	0.05	..	..		50,000,000	0.54	0.96
Hungary	4	4.8	4	4.8	7.1	..			2,174,951,512	2.33	2,174,951,512	2.33	2.47	..	..	..
Iran	3	3.6	2	2.4	3.6	1	1.2	3.7	1,653,000,001	1.77	903,000,000	0.97	1.03	750,000,000	0.8	14.35
Ireland	1	1.2	1	1.2	1.8	..			80,000,000	0.09	80,000,000	0.086	0.09	..	..	..
Israel	4	4.8	3	3.6	5.4	1	1.2	3.7	1,485,000,001	1.59	960,000,000	1	1.09	525,000,000	0.56	10.04
Italy	2	2.4	2	2.4	3.6	..			520,000,000	0.56	520,000,000	0.56	0.59	..	..	..
Kosovo	1	1.2	1	1.2	1.8	..			2,000,000	0.00	2,000,000	0.002	0.00	..	..	..
Latvia	1	1.2	1	1.2	1.8	..			45,000,000	0.05	45,000,000	0.048	0.05	..	..	..
Mexico	5	6.0	2	2.4	3.6	3	3.6	11.1	192,000,000	0.21	52,000,000	0.056	0.06	140,000,000	0.15	2.68
Mozambique	1	1.2		0.0	0.0	1	1.2	3.7	200,000,000	0.21	..	..	..	200,000,000	0.21	3.83
Norway	1	1.2	1	1.2	1.8	..			600,000,000	0.64	600,000,000	0.64	0.68	..	..	..
Romania	1	1.2	1	1.2	1.8	..			5,000,000	0.01	5,000,000	0.005	0.006	..	..	..
Russia	2	2.4	1	1.2	1.8	1	1.2	3.7	36,302,000,041	38.92	36,300,000,000	38.9	41.23	2,000,000	0.002	0.04
Scotland, UK	3	3.6	2	2.4	3.6	1	1.2	3.7	50,000,000	0.05	35,000,000	0.037	0.04	15,000,000	0.016	0.29
South Africa	4	4.8	2	2.4	3.6	2	2.4	7.4	12,113,000,014	12.99	12,000,000,000	12.9	13.63	113,000,000	0.12	2.16
Sweden	1	1.2		0.0	0.0	1	1.2	3.7	20,000,000	0.02	..	..		20,000,000	0.021	0.38
Ukraine	2	2.4	1	1.2	1.8	1	1.2	3.7	50,000,000	0.05	20,000,000	0.021	0.02	30,000,000	0.032	0.57
Venezuela	1	1.2		0.0	0.0	1	1.2	3.7	100,000,000	0.11	..	..		100,000,000	0.11	1.91
Total	83	100.0	56	67.5	100	27	32.5	100.0	93,280,428,114	100.0	88,052,720,525	94.4	100.0	5,227,707,50	5.6	100.00
% of Overall Total		68		45.9	64.4		22.1	77.1		82.3		77.7	82.4		4.6	80.4
Overall Total	122		87	71.3	100	35	28.7	100	113,402,209,064		106,895,048,037	94.3	100	6,507,161,027	5.7	100

Source: Compiled from Forbes Magazine, Celebrity Net Worth, etc. Please see Table A3 in Appendix.

CHAPTER FIVE

DISCUSSION

The data presented above and in the appendixes tell many important stories about the backgrounds and experiences of the "Pride of America" honorees, including their similarities and differences in terms of gender, race, ethnicity, ancestry, month of birth, previous nationality, geography, net worth, and educational attainment. It is useful to note that Brazil (204 million people in 2015) is the only country with 100 million people or more without any former citizens among the "Pride of America" honorees. In a study of the *Times Higher Education*-QS top 200 universities in the world in 2009, not a single institution in Brazil was ranked (Kaba, 2012b, pp.36-46). If Brazil is one large or populous nation that has its people missing in this study, the same can be said for the much smaller countries of Finland and Denmark, given the presence of other Scandinavian nations (e.g., Sweden and Norway) (also see Dutton, 2014).

One important observation pertaining to race and ancestry is what I call "the hidden Asian population in the United States." This refers to categorizing people of Asian descent (e.g., Arabs, Iranians, Israelis or Jews, Afghans, and Turks) in the United States as White, which reduces the overall Asian population in the society. This creates the perception that these honorees are European instead of Asian, because Whiteness is primarily associated with European ancestry. It also puts them in a psychological position whereby they might feel superior to those categorized as Asians, American Indians, or Blacks (Kaba, 2007, pp.13-17; Shapiro, 2013). The United States Federal government is attempting to resolve this issue by creating a new racial categorization called "Middle Eastern and North African" (MENA) for the 2020 United States Census. On September 30, 2016, the White House Office of Management and Budget (OMB) posted a notice in the Federal Register entitled: "Standards for Maintaining, Collecting, and Presenting Federal Data on Race and Ethnicity" for public comment ("Standards for Maintaining, Collecting, and Presenting Federal Data on Race and Ethnicity," 2016). As Korte (2016) writes, this new racial categorization "… would include anyone from a region of the world stretching from

Morocco to Iran, and including Syrian and Coptic Christians, Israeli Jews and other religious minorities."

Table 3 shows that the three months or birth of the "Pride of America" honorees with the highest proportions are January (11%), May (9.8%), and August (9.2%). It is important to note that August is also among the top three months of birth in the United States. For example, according to Martin et al. (2009), of the 4,265,555 births in the United States in 2006, 387,798 (9.1%) were in August, 374,711 (8.8%) were in September, 367,934 (8.6%) were in July, 367,354 (8.6%) were in October, 358,251 (8.4%) were in June, 356,786 (8.4%) were in March, 356,111 (8.3%) were in December, 355,437 (8.3%) were in May, 351,832 (8.2%) were in November, 340,297 (8%) were in January, 329,809 (7.7%) were in April, and 319,235 (7.5%) were in February (p.53). It is noted that "August had the most births each year from 1990 to 2006 except for six years (1992, 1993, 1997, 1998, 2003 and 2004) when it was edged out by July..." (Melina, 2010).

The net worth data of the 122 honorees, which stood at $113.4 billion, is so large that it would rank in the top 81 in 2015 in the CIA World Factbook's rankings of the Gross Domestic Product (GDP) of nations and entities (including the EU) in the world. For example, of the 230 nations and entities ranked in the CIA World Factbook based on their 2015 GDP (as of June 3, 2016), these 122 individuals have more money than the GDP of Ghana ($113.3 billion), ranked number 81 among the 230 nations and entities ("Country Comparison: GDP Purchasing Power Parity," 2016).

As to why there are more male than female honorees, and why higher proportions of male honorees have STEM degrees, one relevant factor might be that there are more foreign-born men than foreign-born women in the United States. That is not the case, at least among naturalized citizens. For example, in 2013 male naturalized citizens in the United States numbered 8,256,000; male non-citizens numbered 11,282,000. For women, naturalized citizens numbered 9,944,000; female non-citizens numbered 10,624,000 ("Table 1.1. Population by Sex, Age, Nativity, and U.S. Citizenship Status: 2013," 2016). The educational attainment gender gap in this study could be connected to wealth accumulation, because it puts male honorees in the position to start a business, earn higher salaries as employees, earn patents, and so on. For example, in 2013, of the 7,551,000 male naturalized citizens aged 25 and above in the United States, 780,000 (10.3%) had master's degrees, 178,000 (2.4%) had professional degrees, and 283,000 (3.8%) had doctorate degrees. For the 9,059,000 male non-citizens, 704,000 (7.8%) had master's degrees, 91,000 (1%) had professional degrees, and 231,000 (2.5%) had doctorate degrees. For the 9,160, 000 female naturalized citizens aged 25 and above in the United States, 825,000 (9%) had master's degrees, 183,000 (2%) had professional degrees, and 142,000 (1.6%) had doctorate degrees. For the 8,692,000 female non-citizens, 540,000 (6.2%) had master's degrees, 80,000 (0.9%) had professional degrees, and 130,000 (1.5%) had doctorate degrees. Of the 82,695,000 native-born males, these rates were 7.6%, 1.9%, and 2%, respectively; for the 89,742,000 native-born females, these rates were 9.2%, 1%, and 1.1%, respectively ("Table 1.5. Educational Attainment of the Population 25 Years," 2016; also see Wai, 2013, p.204).

In 2012, of the 478,000 male foreign-born naturalized citizen family householders with no spouses present in the United States, 97,000 (20.3%) had incomes of $100,000 or more and of the 643,000 male foreign-born non-citizen family householders, 86,000 (13.3%) had incomes of $100,000 or more. 129,000 (10.3%) out of the 1,250,000 of female foreign-born naturalized citizen family householders and 70,000 (5.5%) out of the 1,268,000 foreign-born female non-citizen family householders with no spouses present. The rates of native-born men were 16.3% or 831,000 out of 5,109,000; the rates for native-born women were 9% or 1,162,000 out of 12,950,000. In 2012, 134,000 (14.3%) of the 933,000 male foreign-born naturalized citizen non-family householders in the United States had incomes of $100,000 or more; 120,000 (10.6%) of the 1,133,000 male foreign-born non-citizen non-family householders had incomes of $100,000 or more; 105,000 (8.1%) of the 1,302,000 female foreign-born naturalized citizen non-family householders; 51,000 (6.7%) out of 758,000 foreign-born female non-citizen non-family householders. For native-born males, their rate was 11.7% or 2,075,000 out of 17,682,000; and 6.8% or 1,350,000 out of 19,750,000 for native-born female nonfamily householders ("Table 1.10. Total Money Income of Households by Household Type, Nativity," 2016).

Part of the reason why more male immigrants tend to be successful than their female counterparts is due to the immigration process itself. Shachar and Hirschl (2013) call this "Olympic citizenship," because it offers permanent resident (green card) preference to highly educated or wealthy foreign-born individuals who wish to immigrate to the United States or other wealthy nations. These people are likely to be males: "From the wealthy and highly educated, to top scientists, elite athletes, world-class artists, and successful entrepreneurs and innovators…" (p.73). The United States government, for example, uses its "EB-5" visa category to attract wealthy immigrants. According to Chilea and Kassai (2016), this program's applicant and her or his immediate family members are offered expedited green card process if they: "…invest $1,000,000 or at least $500,000 in a 'Targeted Employment Area' (high unemployment or rural area), creating or preserving at least 10 jobs for U.S. workers excluding the investor and their immediate family" (p.47).

The data provided above show there are more foreign-born women in the United States and there are more naturalized women than are their male counterparts. However, they earn fewer degrees, lower household incomes, and are less recognized. This might be due to the phenomenon of men in the United States, regardless of their racial, ethnic, religious and economic backgrounds, going abroad to seek brides with the promise of American citizenship (e.g., "mail order brides") or marrying immigrant women already in the country who then file for American citizenship (Frates, 2015; Merrimam, 2012; So, 2006). For example, Frates (2015) reports that Melania Trump (from Slovenia) became an American citizen after marrying President Donald Trump in 2005. Although some men come into the United States in this same manner, women far outnumber them.

The data also show that the higher the academic degree level attained, the higher the numbers of earned degrees, especially master's and doctorate degrees (129 doctorates, 92 master's and 76 bachelors). One reason for this is that many immigrants may have arrived with their bachelor's degrees already and attended graduate school in United States. Another factor is that U.S. immigration laws force immigrants to stay in college until they earn their master's, professional, or doctorate degrees. This is because with only a bachelor's degree, they could lose their immigration status due to the difficulty of finding a job. Employers are far more willing to sponsor employees with masters, professional, or doctorate degrees (Kaba, 2007, pp.11-12). Moreover, in the United States, for the most part, immigrants have a good chance of getting employment and higher earnings if they earn a college degree (preferably higher levels) from American as opposed to foreign institutions (Kaushal, 2011, pp.129; Kaba, 2007, pp.21-22).

Most of the institutions listed in this study are also in the top 10, top 25, top 50, top 100, and top 200 ones in the United States and the world (Kaba, 2012b, pp.36-45). One important reason for their dominance in the United States and of some of those abroad (e.g., the University of Oxford) is that they tend to have the characteristics of sovereign states or geographic entities. For example, they have presidents; a president's cabinet; a security or police force; make legal judgments on campus to settle complaints; and have budgets or endowments sometimes more than those of nations; large populations sometimes bigger than towns or cities; and have land or territory. Therefore, even though they are located within states or countries, they have independence in terms of which applicants they will accept. That is why so many of them accept international students. Indeed, at times and perhaps unexpectedly, these institutions give more privileges to international students than to native-born students. For example, the National Science Foundation presents data on various types of primary financial support awarded to 2014 doctorate degree recipients. Of the 14,885 temporary visa holders, 49.9% were awarded research assistantships or traineeships positions; 11% for American Indians, 13.6% for African Americans, 18% for Hispanics, 24.8% for Whites, and 31.4% for Asians ("TABLE 35. Doctorate recipients' primary source of financial support, by broad field of study, sex, citizenship status, ethnicity, and race: 2014," 2016; also see Marvasti, 2007; Weber, 2012).

In 2104, 15,852 temporary residents earned doctorate degrees in the United States, with the top 20 institutions awarding 5,005 (31.6%) of them. Sixteen (80%) of them are listed in this study: #1, Purdue University (376); #2, the University of Illinois, Urbana-Champaign (373); #4, the University of Florida (298); # 6, the University of Michigan; #7, the Georgia Institute of Technology (261); #9, the University of Texas, Austin (246); #10, the Massachusetts Institute of Technology (236); #11, the University of Wisconsin (219); #12, the University of Southern California (216); #13, the University of California, Berkeley (215); #14, Michigan State University (213); #15, Harvard University (211); #16, Virginia Polytechnic Institute and State University (207); #17, the University of Maryland, College Park (196);

#18, Cornell University (194); and #19, Columbia University (190) ("TABLE 10. Top 20 doctorate-granting institutions, ranked by number of doctorate recipients holding temporary visas: 2014," 2016). The study by Wai (2013) examines five influential groups of elites in the United States, with a sample size of 2,254 individuals: Fortune 500 CEOs, federal judges, billionaires, and members of the United States Congress. Two important findings were: (1) men accounted for the majority in each group, and "Within each of these groups, nearly all had attended college with the majority having attended either a highly selective undergraduate institution or graduate school of some kind" (pp.202-203; also see Wai and Rindermann, 2015).

Finally, the data in this study show the predominance of the Northeast and the West (specifically California) in terms of conferring the highest or terminal degrees to the "Pride of America" honorees. In an article examining the appointment of Black American faculty members in the discipline of Education to the position of endowed and distinguished professors, Kaba (2016) finds that both institutions in the Northeast (especially Ivy League institutions) and in the West were underrepresented. This observation was because as this study has demonstrated, these two regions tend to dominate in higher education not just in the United States, but also in the world as a whole. For example, the 8 Ivy League institutions (i.e., Brown University, Cornell University, Dartmouth College, Columbia University, Harvard University, Princeton University, the University of Pennsylvania, and Yale University) are all in the Northeast, are among the country's oldest, and among the institutions with the most money or endowments (a combined endowment of $98.7 billion in 2007) (pp.23-24). California, the country's largest state with 38.8 million people (in 2014), has many of the most prominent higher education institutions, including the University of California, Berkeley, the California Institute of Technology, Stanford University, the University of California, Los Angeles, and the University of Southern California.

The predominance of these two regions is also connected to the fact that most immigrants to the country have headed for and/or settled there (Bankston III, 2007; Donato et al., 2007; Jaret & Kolozsvari-Wright, 2011; Kerr & Lincoln, 2010; Li & Skopf, 2010; Scott et al., 2005). For example, Bankston III (2007) notes that:

> The classic, stereotypical U.S. immigrant destination is a large city in the North, Midwest, or far West. New York, Chicago, San Francisco are fixed in our imaginations as the great American immigrant settlements. Until recently, most people rarely considered the U.S. South when they thought of new arrivals from other countries. For much of American history the South had very few foreign-born people, and from 1850 to 1970, it was home to a smaller percentage of immigrants than any other region.... Even during the great period of migration from 1880 to 1920, a time when massive waves of newcomers arrived on American shores, only about 2.5 percent of the people in the southern states were foreign-born (p.25).

According to Li and Skop (2010), immigrants from China and India have a similar immigration history: "... large numbers of Chinese came as part of the Gold Rush [in California] in the mid-19th century, whereas Indians came down from British Columbia seeking work opportunities in the American Northwest" (p.287). Even though the majority of Black immigrants have, throughout the country's history, resided in the South, in 2013, 41% of all Black immigrants in the United States resided in the Northeast; 41% in the South; and 9% each in the Midwest and West. Even when broken down by region of origin, no Black immigrant group has a majority residing in the South; 25% of Blacks from Africa, 51% of those from the Caribbean, 47% of those from Central America, and 64% of those from South America reside in the Northeast; 40% of Blacks from Africa, 44% of those from the Caribbean, 29% of those from Central America, and 28% of those from South America reside in the South; 19% of Blacks from Africa, 3% of those from the Caribbean, 5% of those from Central America, and 3% of those from South America reside in the Midwest; and finally, 16% of Blacks from Africa, 3% of those from the Caribbean, 19% of those from Central America, and 6% of those from South America reside in the West (Anderson, 2015, pp.21-23. Also see Kerr and Lincoln, 2010, p.489; Scott et al., 2005, p.114).

CHAPTER SIX

CONCLUSION

This paper began by explaining that in the post-World War II era, although immigrants in the United States have experienced various types of negative challenges due to their status, from 2015-2016 the negative tone, extreme criticism, prejudice, and policy proposals of the leading Republican presidential candidates of the Republican Party are among the worst forms of nativism. The paper points to research data illustrating that immigrants in the United States are among the most important taxpayers and employers.

(Re) conceptualizing the brain drain phenomenon as competition, this paper examines the Carnegie Corporation of New York's "Great Immigrants: The Pride of America" honorees from 2006-2015. While many of them emigrated through the traditional brain drain reason (e.g., fleeing poverty, civil conflicts or wars, or ethnic/racial prejudice) the new form of the brain drain is based mostly on competition, with skilled individuals emigrating from very prosperous nations to relocate in the United States – brain drain as competition.

The 408 honorees are in dozens of professions, including journalism, the corporate world, academia, the military, politics, medicine, law, movie or film industry, professional sports, fashion, science, and engineering. Of the 408 honorees, almost 71% are men. Up to two-thirds (66.4%) of them are White, 25% are Asian, and 8% are Black. The months of January, May, and August are their most frequent months of birth. The oldest honoree was born in 1879, and the youngest were born in 1989. Their most common year of birth, with 10 or more, are as follows: 14 (3.6%) each in 1951 and 1955; 12 (3.1%) each in 1949, 1950, 1952, 1956, and 1968; 11 (2.8%) in 1959; and 10 (2.6%) in 1947.

They are from 87 countries or geographic entities, including 10 or more from India, 29 (7.1%); China, 28 (6.9%); England, UK, 22 (5.4%); Canada and Germany each, 20 (4.9%); Iran, 18 (4.4%); Cuba, 17 (4.2%); Mexico, 14 (3.4%); and Israel and Russia each, 13 (3.2%). There are 147 (36%) honorees from Asia (104 men and 43 women), 135 (33.1%) from Europe (96 men and 39 women), 85 (20.8%) from the

Americas (58 men and 27 women), 32 (7.8%) from Africa (26 men and 6 women), and 9 (2.2%) from Oceania (5 men and 4 women).

These individuals are among the most educated people in the United States and the world, with 323 (79.2% of the total 408 honorees) honorees earning 352 highest or terminal degrees combined, from associate degrees to doctorates: 129 (36.7%) doctorate degrees, 92 (26.1%) master's degrees, 76 (21.6%) bachelor's degrees, 30 (8.5%) Juris Doctor degrees (JD), 21 (6%) doctor of medicine degrees (MD), and 4 (1.1%) associate degrees. The most common academic majors are business administration/management, fine arts, economics, physics, engineering, mathematics, computer science, chemistry, and history. A substantial proportion of the degrees were earned from Columbia University, Harvard University, the Massachusetts Institute of Technology, New York University, Princeton University, Stanford University, the University of California, Berkeley, the University of Cambridge, the University of Chicago, the University of Pennsylvania, the University of Southern California, and Yale University.

A very high proportion of the degrees were earned from institutions located in the Northeast, United States, including Massachusetts and New York; and the West, specifically California. The United Kingdom also dominates, with its institutions awarding degrees to these honorees as well.

Finally, available data show that 122 (30% of the total 408 honorees) of these individuals had a total net worth of $113.4 billion: 87 men accounting for $106.9 billion (94.3%), and 35 women for $6.51 billion (5.7%). This total net worth will rank in the top 81 among GDP of countries/geographic entities in the world by June 3, 2016.

Among the nations or countries whose members are missing in this study are Brazil and Finland. The United States' unique racial classifications of people from Asia living in the United States results in a smaller proportion of Asians in this study – a "hidden Asian population in the United States". More men are recognized as great immigrants and have STEM degrees, partly due to the characteristics of United States immigration laws. Finally, the predominance of the Northeast and the West (specifically California) in terms of where academic degrees were earned is due primarily to the fact that the two regions have historically attracted the most immigrants.

REFERENCES

Abel, Ernest L., and Kruger, Michael L. 2010. "Birth Month Affects Longevity," *Death Studies*, 34, (8): 757-763.

Allen, James P. 2006. "How Successful are Recent Immigrants to the United States and Their Children," Yearbook of the Association of Pacific Coast Geographers, 68: 9-32.

Anderson, Monica. 2015, April 9. "A Rising Share of the U.S. Black Population is Foreign Born," Pew Research Center. Retrieved on May 12, 2016 from: http://www.pewsocialtrends.org/2015/04/09/a-rising-share-of-the-u-s-black-population-is-foreign-born/.

"'A Prison is a Prison is a Prison": Mandatory Immigration Detention and The Sixth Amendment Right to Counsel," 2015. Harvard Law Review, 129, (2): 522-543.

Bankston III, Carl L. 2007. "New People in the New South: An Overview of Southern Immigration," *Southern Cultures*, 13, (4): 24-44.

Bideshi, Davison., and Kposowa, Augustine J. 2012. "African Immigrants and Capital Conversion in the U.S. Labor Market: Comparisons by Race and National Origin," *Western Journal of Black Studies*, 36, (3): 181-200.

Black, Amy E., and Rothman, Stanley. 1998. "Have You Really Come a Long Way? Women's Access to Power in the United States," *Gender Issues*, 1, (1): 107-133.

Blanck, Dag. 2014. "'A Mixture of People with Different Roots": Swedish Immigrants in the American Ethno-Racial Hierarchies," *Journal of American Ethnic History*, 33, (3): 37-54.

Boot, Max. 2016. "Is a New Republican Foreign Policy Emerging?" *Commentary*, 141, (2): 11-17.

Bozorgmehr, Mehdi., and Douglas, Daniel. 2011. "Success (ion): Second-Generation Iranian Americans," *Iranian Studies*, 44, (1): 3-24.

Bruner, Jon. 2011, October 5. "American Leadership in Science, Measured in Nobel Prizes," *Forbes Magazine*. Retrieved on November 1, 2015 from: http://www.forbes.com/sites/jonbruner/2011/10/05/nobel-prizes-and-american-leadership-in-science-infographic/#627f66b452a9

Cobb-Clark, Deborah A. 2006. "The Wealth and Asset Holdings of U.S.-Born and Foreign-Born Households: Evidence from SIPP Data," *Review of Income and Wealth*, 52, (1): 17-42.

Campanella, Edoardo. 2015. "Reversing the Elite Brain Drain: A First Step to Address Europe's Skills Shortage," *Journal of International Affairs*, 68, (2): 195-209.

Caprino, Kathy. 2011, October 21. ―Where are the Women on Fortune's ―40 Under 40‖ List?‖ Forbes. Retrieved on January 3, 2012 from: http://www.forbes.com/sites/kathycaprino/2011/10/21/where-are-the-women-on- fortunes-40-under-40-list/

Chavez, Linda. 2015. "Donald Trump's America," *Commentary*, 140, (3): 13-19.

Chilea, Dragos., and Kassai, Christina M. 2016. "Investor Immigration in the U.S.A.: The EB-5 Business Immigration Law," Curentul Juridic, 60: 46-60.

Chopra, Rohit. 2016. "Deoding Ddonald Trump: The Temptations of Populist Democracy," *Economics and Political Weekly*, 11, (4): 23-25.

"Country Comparison: GDP Purchasing Power Parity," 2016. CIA World Factbook. Retrieved on June 5, 2016 from: https://www.cia.gov/library/publications/the world factbook/rankorder/2001rank.html#us.

Delorme, Nicolas., Boiche, Julie., and Raspaud, Michel. 2010. "Relative Age Effect in Elite Sports: Methodological Bias or Real Discrimination?" *European Journal of Sport Science*, 10, (2): 91-96.

Donato, Katharine M., Tolbert II., Charles M., Nucci, Alfred., and Kawano, Yukio. 2007. "Recent Immigrant Settlement in the Nonmetropolitan United States: Evidence from Internal Census Data," *Rural Sociology*, 72, (4): 537-559.

Du, Qianqian., Gao, Hausheng., Levi, Maurice D. 2012. "The Relative-Age Effect and Career Success: Evidence from Corporate CEOs," *Economic Letters*, 117, (3): 660-662.

Edgar, Susan., and O'Donoghue, Peter. 2005. "Season of Birth Distribution of Elite Tennis Players," *Journal of Sports Sciences*, 23, (10): 1013-1020.

"The FP Top Global Thinkers," 2011, December. Retrieve on January 5, 2012 from: http://www.foreignpolicy.com/articles/2011/11/28

/the_fp_top_100_global_thinkers?print=yes&hidecomments=yes&page=full.
Figueroa-Santana, Bianca. 2015. "Divided we Stand: Constitutionalizing Executive Immigration Reform through Subfederal Regulation," *Columbia Law Review*, 115, (8): 2219-2264.
Frates, Chris. 2015, August 24. "Donald Trump's immigrant wives," CNN. Retrieved on December 30, 2015 from:http://www.cnn.com/2015/08/24/politics/donald-trump-immigrant-wives/.
Gaulé, Patrick., and Piacentini, Mario. 2013. "Chinese Graduate Students and U.S. Scientific Productivity," *The Review of Economics and Statistics*, 95, (2): 698-701.
Gonzalez-Barrera, Ana. 2015, July 10. "'Mestizo' and 'mulatto': Mixed-Race Identities Among U.S. Hispanics," Pew Research Center. Retrieved on November 24, 2016 from: http://www.pewresearch.org/fact tank/2015/07/10/mestizo and mulatto mixed race identities-unique-to-hispanics/.
Goutor, David. 2015. "Crossing Borders: National and Theoretical," *Labour / Le Travail*, 76: 199-212.
Greenwood, Michael J., and Ward, Zachary. 2015. "Immigration Quotas, World War I, and Emigrant Flows from the United States in the Early 20th Century," *Explorations in Economic History*, 55: 76-96.
Guo, Jeff. 2015, November 27. "Billionaires Show that Going to a Top College isn't Very Important," *Washington Post*. Retrieved on November 27, 2015 from: https://www.washingtonpost.com/news/wonk/wp/2015/11/27/why-top-journalists-are-better-educated-than-billionaires/
Han, Xueying., Stocking, Galen., Gebbie, Matthew A., Appelbaum, Richard P. 2015. "Will They Stay of Will They Go? International Graduate Students and Their Decisions to Stay or Leave the U.S. upon Graduation," *PLoS ONE*, 10 (3): 1-18.
Hartlet, Nicholas D., Ball, Daisy., Theodosopoulos, Kendra., Wells, Kevin., and Morgan, Grant B. 2016. "A National Analysis of Endowed Chairs and Distinguished Professors in the Field of Education," *Educational Studies*, 52, (2), 119–138.
Hirschl, Ran., and Shachar, 2013. "Recruiting "Super Talent": The New World of Selective Migration Regimes," *Indiana Journal of Global Legal Studies*," 20, (1): 71-107.

Hunt, Jennifer. 2011. "Which Immigrants are Most Innovative and Entrepreneurial? Distinctions by Entry Visa," Journal of Labor Economics, 29, (3): 417-457.

"International Students: Field of Study, 2012-2014," Open Door Data. Institute of International Education. Retrieved on November 4, 2015 from: http://www.iie.org/Research-and-Publications/Open-Doors/Data/International-Students/Fields-of-Study/2012-14.

"International Students: Field of Study by Place of Origin, 2009-2011," 2016. Open Door Data. Institute of International Education. Retrieved on November 4, 2015 from: http://www.iie.org/Research-and-Publications/Open Doors/Data/International Students/Fields-of-Study-Place-of-Origin/2009-10.

International Students in the U.S.: 2015 "Fast Facts,'" 2016. Open Door Data. Institute of International Education. Retrieved on November 4, 2015 from: http://www.iie.org/Research-and-Publications/Open-Doors/Data/Fast-Facts#.V0Rx-jHD_fM.

Jaret, Charles., and Kolozsvari-Wright, Orsolya. 2011. "Citizenship and Naturalization Patterns of Immigrants in the Southeastern United States and their Political Consequences," Norteamérica, 6: 179-208.

Kaba, Amadu Jacky. 2016. "Conceptualizing Tolerance as Recognition: Black American Endowed and Distinguished Professors of Education in US Colleges and Universities," *Sociology Mind*, 6, (1): 1-31.

Kaba, Amadu Jacky. 2015. "Contributors to the American Sociological Review, 2010," *Sociology Mind*, 5, (2): 114-146.

Kaba, Amadu Jacky. 2014. *Monitoring the Health of U.S. Professional Athletes: The Body Mass Index of NBA and WNBA Players, 2005-2006*. London: Adonis & Abbey Publishers Ltd.

Kaba, Amadu Jacky. 2013. *Profile of Contributors to the American Economic Review, 2010: Human Capital Theory, Gender and Race*. Irvine, California: Scientific Research Publishing, Inc.

Kaba, Amadu Jacky. 2012a. "Talented Tenth: An Analysis of the 2011 Root Magazine's 100 Most Influential Young Black Americans," *International Journal of Humanities and Social Science*, 2, (5): 1-31.

Kaba, Amadu Jacky. 2012b. "Analyzing the Anglo-American hegemony in the Times Higher Education Rankings," *Education Policy Analysis Archives*, 20, (21): 1-53.

Kaba, Amadu Jacky. 2011a. "The Status of Africa's Emigration Brain Drain in the 21st Century," *Western Journal of Black Studies*, 35, (3): 187-195.

Kaba, Amadu Jacky. 2011b, June 29. ."Demographics and Publication Productivity of Ivy League Political Science Professors: Harvard, Princeton, University of Pennsylvania and Yale," *Holler Africa Magazine*. http://www.hollerafrica.com/index.php.

Kaba, Amadu Jacky. 2007. "Educational Attainment, Income Levels and Africans in the United States: The Paradox of Nigerian Immigrants," *West Africa Review*, Issue 11:1-27.

Kaba, Amadu Jacky. 2005."Progress of African Americans in Higher Education Attainment: The Widening Gender Gap and Its Current and Future Implications," *Education Policy Analysis Archives*, 13, (25): 1-34.

Kaushal, Neeraj. 2011. "Earning Trajectories of Highly Educated Immigrants: Does Place of Education Matter?" Industrial and Labor Relations Review, 64, (2): 323-340.

Kerr, William R., and Lincoln, William F. "The Supply Side of Innovation: H-B1 Visa Reforms and U.S. Ethnic Invention," *Journal of Labor Economics*, 28, (3): 473-508.

Kim, Dongbin., Wolf-Wendel, Lisa., and Twombly, Susan. 2011. "International Faculty: Experiences of Academic Life and Productivity in U.S. Universities," *The Journal of Higher Education*, 82, (6): 720-747.

Korte, Gregory. 2016, September 30. "White House wants to add new racial category for Middle Eastern people," USA Today. Retrieved on October 5, 2016 from: http://www.usatoday.com/story/news/politics/2016/09/30/whie house wants add new racial category middle easternpeople/91322064/.

Lal, Vinay. 2015. "Implications of American Islamophobia," *Economics and Political Weekly*, 1, (51): 12-14.

Li, Wei., and Skop, Emily. 2010. "Diaspora in the United States: Chinese and Indians Compared," *Journal of Chinese Overseas*," 6, (2): 286-310.

Lyytinen, K., Baskerville, R., Livari, J., and Te'eni, D. 2007. "Why the Old World Cannot Publish? Overcoming Challenges in Publishing High-Impact IS Research," *European Journal of International Systems*, 16, (4): 317-326.

Manieri, Maureen. 2015, October 27. "Quarterly Publication of Individuals, Who Have Chosen to Expatriate, as Required by Section 6039G," *Federal Register*, 80, (207): 65851-65870.
Martin, Joyce A., Hamilton, Brady E., Sulton, Paul D., Ventura, Stephanie J., Menacker, Fay., Kirmeyer, Sharon., and Mathews, T.J. 2009. "Births: Final Data for 2006," *National Vital Statistics Reports*, 57, (7): 1-104.
Marvasti, Akbar. 2007. "Foreign-Born Teaching Assistants and Student Achievement: An Ordered Probit Analysis," *American Economist*, 51, (2): 61-71.
McDowell, John M., and Singell., Jr., Larry D. "Productivity of Highly Skilled Immigrants: Economists in the Postwar Period," *Economic Inquiry*, 38, (4): 672-684.
Melina, Remy. 2010, July 27. "In Which Month are the Most Babies Born?" Livescience. Retrieved on May 18, 2016 from: http://www.livescience.com/32728-baby-month-is-almost-here-.html.
Merriman, Justin S. 2012. "Holy Matrimony Plus Shipping and Handling A Libertarian Perspective on the Mail-Order Bride Industry," *Independent Review*, 17, (1): 81-93.
Michopoulos, Aris. 2013. "The Greek Immigration to the United States: Yesterday and Today," *Hellenic Studies*, 21, (2): 47-78.
Newlove, Russell. 2016, February. "Why Expat Americans are Giving up their Passports," bbc.com. Retrieved on April 23, 2016 from: http://www.bbc.com/news/35383435.
No, Yeonji., and Walsh, John P. 2010. "The Importance of Foreign-born Talent for US Innovation," *Nature Biotechnology*, 28, (3): 289-291.
"Nobel Prizes 2015," 2015. Retrieved on February 4, 2016 from: http://www.nobelprize.org/nobel_prizes/lists/year/index.html?year=2015&images=yes.
Ornstein, Allan. 2015. "The Search for Talent," *Society*, 52, (2): 142-149.
Painter II, Matthew A. 2015. "Social Capital and Immigrant Wealth Inequality: Visa Sponsorship and the Role of Ties, Education, and Race/Ethnicity," *Research in Social Stratification and Mobility*, 42: 62-72.
"People Reporting Ancestry, Universe: Total Population 2014 American Survey 1-Year Estimates," 2016. American Fact Finder. United States Census Bureau. Retrieved on June 12, 2016 from:

http://factfinder.census.gov/faces/tableservices/jsf/pages/productview.xhtml?src=CF.

Petras, James. 2008. "Global Ruling Class: Billionaires and How They "Make It,'" *Journal of Contemporary Asia*, 38, (2): 319-329.

Peri, Giovanni., and Sparber, Chad. 2011. "Highly Educated Immigrants and Native Occupational Choice," *Industrial Relations*, 50, (3): 385-411.

Rodriguez, Leila. 2014. "The Transnational Political Involvement of Nigerian Immigrants in New York City: Motivations, Means and Constraints," *Journal of International and Global Studies*, 6, (1): 50-71.

Ross, Janell. 2015, November 3. "A Record Number of Americans are Renouncing their Citizenship. What's Going on Here?" *Washington Post*. Retrieved on May 23, 2016 from: https://www.washingtonpost.com/news/the-fix/wp/2015/11/03/a-record-number-of-americans-are renouncing-their-citizenship-whats-going-on-here/.

Rubinoff, Arthur, G. 2005. "The Diaspora as a Factor in U.S.-Indian Relations," *Asian Affairs*, 32, (3): 169-187.

Saxenian, AnnaLee. 2002. "Brain Circulation: How High-Skill Immigration Makes Everyone Better Off," The Brookings Review, 20, (1): 28-31.

Scott, Darren M., Coomes, Paul A., and Izyumov, Alexei I. 2005. "The Location Choice of Employment-Based Immigrants Among U.S. Metro Areas," *Journal of Regional Science*, 45, (1): 113-145.

Shachar, Ayelet. 2011. "Picking Winners: Olympic Citizenship and the Global Race for Talent," *The Yale Law Journal*, 12, (8): 2088-2139.

Shachar, Ayelet., and Hirschl, Ran. 2013. "Recruiting "Super Talent": The New World of Selective Migration Regimes," *Indiana Journal of Global Legal Studies*, 20, (1): 71-107.

Shapiro, Edward. 2013. "The Absent American Jewish Business Mogul," *Society*, 50, (3): 293-300.

Shenoy-Packer, Suchitra. 2015. "Immigrant Professionals, Microaggressions, and Critical Sensemaking in the U.S. Workforce," *Management Communication Quarterly*, 29, (2): 257-275.

So, Christine. 2006. "Asian Mail-Order Brides, the Threat of Global Capitalism, and the Rescue of the U.S. Nation-State," *Feminist Studies*, 32, (1): 395-419.

"Standards for Maintaining, Collecting, and Presenting Federal Data on Race and Ethnicity," 2016, September 30. United States Federal

Register. Federal Register Number: 2016-23672. Retrieved on October 1, 2016 from: https://www.regulations.gov/document?D=OMB-2016-0002-0001.

Suchan, Trudy A., Perry, Marc J., Fitzsimmons, James D., Juhn, Anika E., Tait, Alexander M., and Brewer, Cynthia A. 2007. "Census Atlas of the United States," United States Census Bureau. Retrieved on January 3, 2016 from: https://www.census.gov/population/www/cen2000/censusatlas/.

"Table 1.1. Population by Sex, Age, Nativity, and U.S. Citizenship Status: 2013," 2016. Current Population Survey - 2013 Detailed Tables. U.S Census Bureau. Retrieved on May 22, 2016 from: http://www.census.gov/population/foreign/data/cps2013.html.

"Table 1.5. Educational Attainment of the Population 25 Years and Over by Sex, Nativity, and U.S. Citizenship Status: 2013," 2016. Current Population Survey - 2013 Detailed Tables. U.S Census Bureau. Retrieved on May 22, 2016 from: http://www.census.gov/population/foreign/data/cps2013.html.

"Table 1.10. Total Money Income of Households by Household Type, Nativity of the Householder, and U.S. Citizenship Status of the Householder: 2012," 2016. Current Population Survey - 2013 Detailed Tables. U.S Census Bureau. Retrieved on May 22, 2016 from: http://www.census.gov/population/foreign/data/cps2013.html.

"TABLE 10. Top 20 doctorate-granting institutions, ranked by number of doctorate recipients holding temporary visas: 2014," 2016. Science and Engineering Doctorates. National Science Foundation. Retrieved on April 30, 2016 from: http://www.nsf.gov/statistics/2016/nsf16300/data/tab10.pdf.

"TABLE 17. Doctorate recipients, by citizenship status and broad field of study: Selected years, 1984–2014,"2016. Science and Engineering Doctorates. National Science Foundation. Retrieved on April 30, 2016 from: http://www.nsf.gov/statistics/2016/nsf16300/data/tab17.pdf.

"TABLE 35. Doctorate recipients' primary source of financial support, by broad field of study, sex, citizenship status, ethnicity, and race: 2014," 2016. Science and Engineering Doctorates. National Science Foundation.

Retrieved on April 30, 2016 from: http://www.nsf.gov/statistics/2016/nsf16300/data/tab35.pdf.

"TABLE 53. Doctorate recipients with temporary visas intending to stay in the United States after doctorate receipt, by country of citizenship: 2008–14," Science and Engineering Doctorates. National Science Foundation. Retrieved on April 30, 2016 from: http://www.nsf.gov/statistics/2016/nsf16300/data/tab53.pdf.

Teich, Albert H. 2014. "Streamlining the Visa and Immigration Systems for Scientists and Engineers," *Issues in Science and Technology*, XXXI, (1): 55-64.

Timberlake, Jeffrey M., and Williams, Rhys H. 2012. "Stereotypes of U.S. Immigrants from Four Global Regions," *Social Science Quarterly*, 93, (4): 867-890.

Wai, Jonathan. 2013. "Investigating America's Elite: Cognitive Ability, Education, and Sex Differences," *Intelligence*, 41, (4):203-211.

Wai, Jonathan., and Rindermann, Heiner. 2015. "The Path and Performance of a Company Leader: A Historical Examination of the Education and Cognitive Ability of Fortune 500 CEOs," *Intelligence*, 53: 102-107.

Webber, Karen L. 2012. "Research Productivity of Foreign-and US-Born Faculty: Differences by Time on Task," *Higher Education*, 64, (5): 709-729.

Wood, Robert W. 2015, October 26. "Reverse Immigration: Americans Renounce Citizenship in Record Numbers," Forbes Magazine. Retrieved on April 23, 2016 from: http://www.forbes.com/sites/robertwood/2015/10/26/reverse-immigration-americans-renounce-citizenship-in-record-numbers/#221b643b4079.

Young, Patrick. 2015, October 7. "Aziz Sancar, a Second Immigrant to Win a Nobel Prize," *Long Island Wins*. Retrieved on November 30, 2015 from:

http://www.longislandwins.com/news/detail/aziz_sancar_a_second_immigrant_to_win_a_nobel_prize

Ziabari, Kourosh. 2016. "Donald Trump, Muslims and the Constitution: Q&A with Tayyib Rashid," *International Policy Digest*, 3, (1): 23-27.

Ziabari, Kourosh. 2016. "Mr. Trump! We are Muslims, Not Monsters," *International Policy Digest*, 3, (1): 69-70.

Zong, Jie., and Batalova, Jeanne. 2016, April 14. "Frequently Requested Statistics on Immigrants and Immigration in the United States,"

Migration Policy.org. Retrieved on May 15, 2016 from: http://www.migrationpolicy.org/article/frequently-requested-statistics-immigrants-and-immigration-united-states#Naturalization Trends

Zong, Jie., and Batalova, Jeanne. 2016, January 6. "Asian Immigrants in the United States," Migration Policy.org. Retrieved on May 15, 2016 from: http://www.migrationpolicy.org/article/asian-immigrants-united-states#Immigration Pathways and Naturalization.

APPENDIXES

Table A1. Name, Previous Country/Nationality, and Profession of Carnegie Corporation's "Pride of America" Honorees, 2006-2015
N=408

Women (n=119)		
Name	Previous Country/Nationality	Profession
Einat Admony	Israel	Chef/Restaurateur
Madeleine Albright	Czech Republic	Diplomat
Isabel Allende	Peru	Author
Goli Ameri	Iran	President and CEO of the Center for Global Engagement
Anousheh Ansari	Iran	Co-founder and CEO of Prodea Systems
Liz Balmaseda	Cuba	Pulitzer Prize-Winning Journalist
Bette Bao Lord	China	Author, Human Rights Advocate, Philanthropist
Rosemary Barkett	Mexico	Judge, Iran-United States Claims Tribunal
Lidia Bastianich	Croatia	Chef
Monika Bauerlein	Germany	Journalist
Cristina V. Beato	Cuba	Deputy Director of the Pan American Health Organization
Elizabeth Blackburn	Australia	Biologist and Nobel Laureate
Louise Bourgeois	France	Sculptor
Geraldine Brooks	Australia	Pulitzer Prize-winning Author and Journalist
Safra Catz	Israel	Co-President and CFO of Oracle
Elaine Chao	Taiwan	Public Service
Rabia Chaudry	Pakistan	Attorney and Civil Rights Activist
JuJu Chang	South Korea	Journalist
Cristeta Comerford	Philippines	Executive Chef of the White House
Maria Contreras-Sweet	Mexico	Administrator, U.S. Small Business Administrator
Edwidge Danticat	Haiti	Author

Table A1 continues…

Women (n=119)		
Name	Previous Country/Nationality	Profession
Cheryl Diaz Meyer	Philippines	Photographer
Sheena Easton	Scotland, UK	Singer
Mica Ertegun	Romania	Interior Designer, Philanthropist
Gloria Estefan	Cuba	Singer
Daisy Expósito-Ulla	Cuba	President and CEO of d eExpósito & Partners
Varsovia Fernandez	Dominican Republic	President and CEO of the Greater Philadelphia Hispanic Chamber of Commerce
Ping Fu	China	Entrepreneur
Jennifer Granholm	Canada	Politician
Sophia Grojsman	Belarus	Performer
Noosheen Hashemi	Iran	Philanthropist
Salma Hayek	Mexico	Actor
Le Ly Hayslip	Vietnam	Author and Philanthropist
Teresa Heinz	Mozambique	Philanthropist
Carolina Herrera	Venezuela	Fashion Designer
Maria Hinojosa	Mexico	Broadcast Journalist
Mazie Hirono	Japan	U.S. Senator
Manuela Hoelterhoff	Germany	Executive Editor, Bloomberg Muse at Bloomberg
Hanna Holborn Gray	Germany	Educator/Professor Emerita, University of Chicago
Ariannna Huffington	Greece	Chair, President, and Editor-in-Chief of the Huffington Post
Ayesha Jalal	Pakistan	Scholar
Marie-Josée Kravis	Canada	Economist, Philanthropist
Andrea Jung	Canada	President and CEO of Grameen America
Joyce L. Kennard	Indonesia	Retired Associate Justice, California Supreme Court
Jill Ker Conway	Australia	Historian
Porochista Khakpour	Iran	Author

Table A1 continues...

Women (n=119)		
Name	**Previous Country/Nationality**	**Profession**
Renu Khator	India	Chancellor of the University of Houston System
Nina Khrushcheva	Russia	Scholar and Editor
Mari Kimura	Japan	Violinist
Jamaica Kincaid	Antigua & Barbuda	Author
Maria Klawe	Canada	President of Harvey Mudd College
Heidi Klum	Germany	Fashion Model
Madeleine M. Kunin	Switzerland	Politician
Mila Kunis	Ukraine	Actress
Maria Elena Lagomasino	Cuba	Business Leader
Jhumpa Lahiri	England, UK	Author
Angela Lansbury	England, UK	Actress
Bai Ling	China	Actor
Nastia Liukin	Russia	U.S. Olympic Medal-winning Gymnast
Lara Logan	South Africa	Broadcast Journalist
Ann-Margret	Sweden	Actress
Kati Marton	Hungary	Author
Franziska Michor	Austria	Vilcek Prize-winning Professor, Computational Biology
Anchee Min	China	Author
Jenny Ming	China	President and CEO of Charlotte Russe
Iman Mohamed Abdulmajid	Somalia	Fashion Model
Sharmin Mossavar-Rahmani	Iran	Chief Investment Officer of the Private Wealth Management Group, Goldman Sachs
Mee Moua	Laos	President of Asian Americans Advancing Justice
Elsa Murano	Cuba	Educator
Azar Nafisi	Iran	Author, Scholar
Josie Natori	Philippines	Fashion Designer and Philanthropist

Table A1 continues...

Women (n=119)		
Name	Previous Country/Nationality	Profession
Martina Navrotilova	Czech Republic	Tennis Player
Shirin Neshat	Iran	Artist
Loida Nicolas-Lewis	Philippines	Chair and CEO of TLC Beatrice and Philanthropist
Indra Nooyi	India	Chair and CEO of PepsiCo
Maureen O'Hara	Ireland	Actress
Yoko Ono	Japan	Conceptual Artist
Maria Otero	Bolivia	Former U.S. Under Secretary of State for Civilian Security, Democracy & Human Rights
Neri Oxman	Israel	Vilcek Prize Winner, Design
Elena Pirozhkova	Russia	Olympic Wrestling Champion
Paulina Porizkova	Czech Republic	Fashion Model
Dina Powell	Egypt	President of the Goldman Sachs Foundation
Samantha Power	Ireland	Ambassador
Sara Ramirez	Mexico	Actress
Helen Reddy	Australia	Singer
Sanya Richards-Ross	Jamaica	Track and Field Athlete
Heana Ros-Lehtinen	Cuba	U.S. Congresswoman
Hana Rovner	Latvia	Judge, U.S. Court of Appeals, Seventh Circuit
Pardis Sabeti	Iran	Vilcek Prize Winner, Biomedical Science
Nadja Salerno-Sonnenberg	Italy	Violinist
Denise Scott Brown	Zambia	Architect
Renata Scotto	Italy	Opera Singer
Meryle Secrest	England, UK	Biographer
Bapsi Sidhwa	Pakistan	Author
Maria Siemionow	Poland	Scientist
Madhulika Sikka	India	VP & Executive Editor, Mic
Ariadna Thalía Sodi-Miranda Mottola	Mexico	Singer, Actress

Table A1 continues…

Women (n=119)		
Name	Previous Country/Nationality	Profession
Melanie Stiassny	Germany	Ichthyologist
Shirin Tahir-Kheli	India	Ambassador
Vivienne Tam	China	Fashion Designer
Ann Telnaes	Sweden	Pulitzer Prize-winning Political Cartoonist
Charlize Theron	South Africa	Actress
Alice Y. Ting	Taiwan	Chemist
Isabel Toledo	Cuba	Fashion Designer
Tuyen Tran	Vietnam	Vilcek Prize-winning Fashion Designer
Monique Truong	Vietnam	Author
Tracy Ullman	England, UK	Actress
Sofia Vergara	Colombia	Actress, Director
Lillian Vernon	Germany	Founder, Lillian Vernon Corporation
Nora Volkow	Mexico	Director of the National Institute on Drug Abuse
Gordana Vunjak-Novakovic	Serbia	Biomedical Engineer
Padmasree Warrior	India	Chief Strategy and Technology Officer of Cisco Systems
Gerda Weissmann Klein	Poland	Author
Anna Wintour	England, UK	Editor-in-Chief of Vogue
Flossie Wong-Staal	China	Virologist
Joanna Wysocka	Poland	Biochemist
Doualy Xaykaothao	Laos	Journalist
Yulia Zagoruychenko	Russia	Dancer
Huda Zoghbi	Lebanon	Neurologist

Men (n=289)		
André Aciman	Egypt/Italy*	Author
Hesanmi Adesida	Nigeria	Vice Chancellor for Academic Affairs and Provost at the University of Illinois, Urbana Champain

Table A1 continues…

Women (n=119)		
Name	Previous Country/Nationality	Profession
Freddy Adu	Ghana	Soccer Player
Ralph Alvarez	Cuba	Business Leader
Cyrus Amir-Mokri	Iran	Assistant Secretary for Financial Institutions, U.S. Treasury Department
Louis van Amstel	Netherlands	Dancer/Choreographer
José Andrés	Spain	Chef
Mario Andretti	Italy	Race Car Driver
Paul Anka	Canada	Recording Artist
Joseph Aoun	Lebanon	President, Northeastern University
Kofi Appenteng	Ghana	Chairman of the Africa-America Institute and International Center for Transitional Justice
Michael Arad	Israel	Architect
Maurice Ashley	Jamaica	Chess Grandmaster
Isaac Asimov	Russia	Author
Reza Aslan	Iran	Author/Religion Scholar
Roy L. Austin	St. Vincent and the Grenadines	Former U.S. Ambassador to Trinidad and Tobago
Arsen Avakian	Armenia	CEO and Co-Founder, Argo Tea
Ramani Ayer	India	Business Leader
Ralph Baer	Germany	National Medal of Technology and Innovation Winner, Inventor
Leonardo Balada	Spain	Composer
Mikhail Baryshnikov	Latvia	Dancer
Mohamad Bazzi	Lebanon	Journalist
Carlos Tiburcio Bea	Spain	Judge of U.S. Court of Appeals for the 9th Circuit
Ishmael Beah	Sierra Leone	Author
Preet Bharara	Indian	U.S. Attorney, Southern District of New York
Jamshed Bharucha	India	Neuroscientist
Hamid Biglari	Iran	Banker and Strategic Thinker

Table A1 continues...

Women (n=119)		
Name	Previous Country/Nationality	Profession
Theodore Bikel	Austria	Actor
Simon Billinge	England, UK	Physicist
Robert Birgeneau	Canada	Chancellor of the University of California, Berkeley
Günter Blobel	Germany	Biologist and Nobel Laureate
W. Michael Blumenthal	Germany	Politician
Bert Blyleyen	Netherlands	Baseball Player
Rudolph Boschwitz	Germany	Former U.S. Senator from Minnesota
Willard Boyle	Canada	Physicist and Nobel Laureate
Sergey Brin	Russia	Co-Founder of Google and Philanthropist
Martin Brodeur	Canada	Hockey Player
Yefim Bronfman	Uzbekistan	Pianist
Pierce Brosnan	Ireland	Actor
Zbigniew Brzezinski	Poland	Foreign Policy Advisor
Carlos Bustamante	Peru	Biophysicist
Semyon Bychkov	Russia	Conductor
Thomas Campbell	England, UK	Director and CEO, The Metropolitan Museum of Art
Andrés Cantor	Argentina	Sportscaster
Anh "Joseph" Cao	Vietnam	Politician
Gerhard Casper	Germany	Scholar
Gregory Chamitoff	Canada	Astronaut
Franklin Chang-Diaz	Costa Rica	Founder and President of AD Astra Rocket Company
Steve Chen	Taiwan	Entrepreneur In Residence, Google Ventures
Denny Chin	Hong Kong, China	Federal Judge
John Cho	South Korea	Actor
Deepak Chopra	India	Author
Howard Chua-Eoan	Philippines	Journalist
Andrei Codrescu	Romania	Author

Table A1 continues...

Women (n=119)		
Name	**Previous Country/Nationality**	**Profession**
Alan Cumming	Scotland, UK	Actor
Samuel Der-Yeghiayan	Syria	Federal Judge
Junot Diaz	Dominican Republic	Author
Viet Dinh	Vietnam	Legal Scholar
Carl Djerassi	Austria	Chemist
Tony Dovolani	Kosovo	Dancer
Tan Dun	China	Composer/Conductor; Global Goodwill Ambassador, UNESCO
Freeman Dyson	England, UK	Physicist
Victor Dzau	China	President of the Institute of Medicine
Albert Einstein	Germany	Physicist and Nobel Laureate
Farouk El-Baz	Egypt	Geologist
Jaime Escalante	Bolivia	Educator
A. Gabriel Esteban	Philippines	President of Seton Hall University
Harold Evans	England, UK	Editor
Patrick Ewing	Jamaica	Basketball Player
Tariq Farid	Pakistan	Co-founder and CEO of Edible Arrangements
Nariman Farvardin	Iran	President of Stevens Institute of Technology
Craig Ferguson	Scotland, UK	Television Host
Stanley Fischer	Israel	Economist; Vice Chair, Board of Governors, Federal Reserve
C. Michael Foale	England, UK	Astronaut
Milos Forman	Czech Republic	Film Director
Michael J. Fox	Canada	Actor and Philanthropist
Adonal Foyle	Saint Vincent and the Grenadines	Basketball Player and Humanitarian
Peter Frampton	England, UK	Recording Artist
Max Frankel	Germany	Journalist
John L. Fugh	China	Major General, U.S. Military
Ric Fulop	Venezuela	Entrepreneur

Table A1 continues...

Women (n=119)		
Name	**Previous Country/Nationality**	**Profession**
Andy Garcia	Cuba	Actor
Patrick Gaspard	Haiti**	U.S. Ambassador to South Africa
Frank Gehry	Canada	Architect
Yousif B. Ghafari	Lebanon	Ambassador and Philanthropist
Riccardo Giacconi	Italy	Physicist and Nobel Laureate
Ivar Giaever	Norway	Nobel Prize Winner, Physics
Osvaldo Golijov	Argentina	Composer
Emilio T. Gonzalez	Cuba	Director of the Miami-Dade Aviation Department
Stanley Gorene	Slovenia	U.S. Military General
Wayne Gretzky	Canada	Hockey Player
Andrew S. Grove	Hungary	Business Leader and Philanthropist
Roger Guillemin	France	Nobel Prize Winner, Medicine
Rajat Gupta	India	Business Leader
Carlos Gutierrez	Cuba	Chairman of Albright Stonebridge Group
Albert O. Hirschman	Germany	Economist
Christopher Hitchens	England, UK	Journalist
David Ho	Taiwan	Scientific Director and CEO of Aaron Diamond AIDS Research Center
Khaled Hosseini	Afghanistan	Author and Physician
Djimon Hounsou	Benin	Actor
Jonathan Hunt	England, UK	Fox News Correspondent
Martin Indyk	England, UK	Diplomat
Malek Jandali	Syria	Composer, Pianist
Christo Vladimirov Javacheff	Bulgaria	Visual Artist
Jacques Jiha	Haiti	Commissioner, NYC Dept. of Finance
Ha Jin	China	Author
Gata Kamsky	Russia	Chess Grandmaster

Table A1 continues...

Women (n=119)		
Name	Previous Country/Nationality	Profession
Eric Kandel	Austria	Neuroscientist and Nobel Laureate
Sukhee Kang	South Korea	Politicians
Yibin Kang	China	Biologist
Charles K. Kao	China	Physicist and Nobel Laureate
Fred Kavli	Norway	Physicist and Philanthropist
M. Farooq Kathwari	India	Chairman, President, and CEO of Ethan Allen Interiors
Lubomir Kavalek	Czech Republic	Chess Grandmaster
Meb Keflezighi	Eritrea	Marathon Runner
Melikset Khachiyan	Azerbaijan	Chess Grandmaster
Zalmay Khalilzad	Afghanistan	Diplomat
Har Gobind Khorana	India	Chemist and Nobel Laureate
Vinod Khosla	India	Entrepreneur
Rakesh Khurana	India	Danoff Dean of Harvard College & Marvin Bower Professor of Leadership & Development
Sergei Khrushchev	Russia	Scholar
Daniel Dae Kim	South Korea	Actor
Jim Yong Kim	South Korea	President of the World Bank
Henry Kissinger	Germany	Diplomat and Nobel Laureate
John W. Kluge	Germany	Entrepreneur and Philanthropist
Walter Kohn	Austria	Physicist and Nobel Laureate
Ted Koppel	England, UK	Broadcast Journalist
Michael Kouakou	Cote d'Ivoire	Dancer
Vivek Kundra	India	Federal Chief Information Officer
George Walter Landau	Austria	Former U.S. Ambassador to Paraguay, Chile, and Venezuela
Bernard Lagat	Kenya	Track-and-Field Runner
Tom Lantos	Hungary	Politician
Peter Lax	Hungary	Mathematician
Ang Lee	Taiwan	Film Director

Table A1 continues...

Women (n=119)		
Name	Previous Country/Nationality	Profession
Chang-Rae Lee	South Korea	Author
Chong-Moon Lee	South Korea	Business Leader and Philanthropist
Tsung-Dao Lee	China	Physicist and Nobel Laureate/Professor
John Alberto Leguizamo	Colombia	Actor
Ivan Lendl	Czech Republic	Tennis Player
Rich Little	Canada	Impressionist/Actor/Comedian
John Liu	Taiwan	Politician
Wallace Loh	China	President of the University of Maryland, College Park
Lopez Lomong	South Sudan	Track-and-Field Runner
Zhou Long	China	Pulitzer Prize-Winning Composer
Bernard Lown	Lithuania	Physician and Nobel Laureate
Michael Lopez-Alegria	Spain	President of the Commercial Spaceflight Federation
Ranan R. Lurie	Egypt	Political Cartoonist
Yo-Yo Ma	France	Cellist
Robert MacNeil	Canada	Broadcast Journalist
Vincent Mai	South Africa	Chairman and CEO of Cranemere LLC
Ali Maleksadeh	Iran	President, Roosevelt University
Hermit Singh Malik	India	Biologist
Asif Mandvi	India	Actor/Comedian
Melquiades Martinez	Cuba	Chairman of the Southeast U.S. and Latin America for JP Morgan Chase & Co.
Pedro Martinez	Dominican Republic	Baseball Player
Joan Massagué	Spain	Director of the Sloan-Kettering Institute
Dave Matthews	South Africa	Singer-Songwriter
Alejandro Mayorkas	Cuba	Deputy Secretary of Homeland Security
Colum McCann	Ireland	Author

Table A1 continues...

Women (n=119)		
Name	**Previous Country/Nationality**	**Profession**
Michael McRobbie	Australia	President of Indiana University
Eliseo Medina	Mexico	Intl. Secretary-Treasurer of the Service Employees Intl. Union
Robert Mehrabian	Iran	President and CEO of Teledyne Technologies
Dinaw Mengestu	Ethiopia	Author
Paul Merage	Iran	Entrepreneur and Philanthropist
Ioannis (Yannis) N. Miaoulis	Greece	President and Director of the Museum of Science in Boston
Lorne Michaels	Canada	TV producer
Mario Molina	Mexico	Chemist and Nobel Laureate
Philippe de Montebello	France	Museum Director
Paul Muldoon	Ireland	Poet
Rupert Murdoch	Australia	Publisher
Elon Musk	South Africa	Entrepreneur and Philanthropist
Dikembe Mutombo	Dem. Rep. of Congo	Basketball player and Philanthropist
Mike Myers	Canada	Actor
Satya Nadella	India	CEO, Microsoft
Firouz Michael Naderi	Iran	Director, Solar System Exploration, NASA Jet Propulsion Laboratory
Yoichiro Nambu	Japan	Nobel Prize Winner, Physics
Vali Nasr	Iran	Dean of Johns Hopkins School of Advanced International Studies
Joseph Neubauer	Israel	Business Leader and Philanthropist
Craig Nevill-Manning	New Zealand	Engineering Director, Google
Mike Nichols	Germany	Film and Theater Director
Chrysostomos L. Max Nikias	Cyprus	President of the University of Southern California
Kojo Nnamdi	Guyana	Broadcast Journalist
Nitin Nohria	India	Dean of Harvard Business School
Carlos Noriega	Peru	Astronaut
Eduado Ochoa	Argentina	President of California State University, Monterey Bay

Table A1 continues...

Women (n=119)		
Name	Previous Country/Nationality	Profession
Masi Oka	Japan	Actor
Hakeem Olajuwon	Nigeria	Basketball Player
Claes Oldenburg	Sweden	Sculptor
Pierre Omidyar	France	Founder of eBay and Philanthropist
David J. O'Reilly	Ireland	Business Leader
David Ortiz	Dominican Republic	Baseball Player
Frank Oz	England, UK	Puppeteer
Eduardo J. Padrón	Cuba	President of Miami Dade College
Vikram Pandit	India	Executive Chairman of TGG
Thakoon Panichgul	Thailand	Fashion Designer
Constantine Papadakis	Greece	Educator
Raj Patel	England, UK	Sociologist
I.M. Pei	China	Architect
Cesar Pelli	Argentina	Architect
Feniosky Peña-Mora	Dominican Republic	Educator
Eddie Perez	Venezuela	Bullpen Coach, Atlanta Braves
Itzhak Perlman	Israel	Violinist
Gholam Peyman	Iran	National Medal of Technology and Innovation Winner, Ophthalmologist
Andre Previn	Germany	Composer
Albert Pujols	Dominican Republic	Baseball Player
Mohammad H. Qayoumi	Afghanistan	President of San Jose State University
Alfredo Quinones-Hinojosa	Mexico	Neurosurgeon
Safi Qureshey	Pakistan	Entrepreneur
Jorge Ramos	Mexico	News Anchor
L. Rafael Reif	Venezuela	President of Massachusetts Institute of Technology
Oscar de la Renta	Dominican Republic	Fashion Designer and Philanthropist
Ciro Rodriguez	Mexico	Politician
Felix G. Rohatyn	Austria	Investment Banker

Table A1 continues...

Women (n=119)		
Name	**Previous Country/Nationality**	**Profession**
Nouriel Roubini	Turkey	Economist
Hector Ruiz	Mexico	CEO of Advanced Nanotechnology Solutions
Morley Safer	Canada	Broadcast Journalist
Roald Sagdeev	Russia	Physicist
Abuhena Saifulislam	Bangladesh	Navy Chaplain
Marcus Samuelson	Ethiopia	Chef
Arturo Sandoval	Cuba	Grammy Award-winning Jazz and Classical Trumpeter
Carlos Santana	Mexico	Guitarist
Fayez Sarofim	Egypt	Investor and Philanthropist
Arnold Schwarzenegger	Austria	Actor
Beheruz Sethna	India	President Emeritus, University of West Georgia
John Shalikashvili	Poland	General, U.S. Military
Harold T. Shapiro	Canada	Economist/Former President of Princeton
Simon Shmueli	Israel	Inventor
Gary Shteyngart	Russia	Author
M. Night Shyamalan	India	Film Director
Charles Simic	Yugoslavia/Serbia	Poet
Dimitri Simes	Russia	President and CEO of the Center for the National Interest
Dumarsais Siméus	Haiti	Entrepreneur and Philanthropist
Gene Simmons	Israel	Bass Guitarist
Charles Simonyi	Hungary	Computer Scientist and Philanthropist
Yakov Smirnoff	Ukraine	Actor
Albio Sires	Cuba	U.S. Congressman
Oliver Smithies	England, UK	Geneticist and Nobel Laureate
Patrick Soon-Shiong	South Africa	Medical Researcher and Philanthropist
George Soros	Hungary	Financier and Philanthropist

Table A1 continues…

Women (n=119)		
Name	Previous Country/Nationality	Profession
Sree Sreenivasan	India	Chief Digital Officer of the Metropolitan Museum of Art
Sri Srinivasan	India	Judge of U.S. Court of Appeals, D.C. Circuit
Thomas C. Südhof	Germany	Nobel Prize-winning Professor of Neuroscience, Physician
Subra Suresh	India	President, Carnegie Mellon University
Jack Szostak	England, UK	Biochemist and Nobel Laureate
Elie Tahari	Israel	Fashion Designer
Oscar Tang	China	Business Leader and Philanthropist
Antonio M. Tauguba	Philippines	U.S. Army Major General, Retired
Sidney Taurel	Morocco	Business Leader
Aso O. Tavitian	Bulgaria	Business Leader and Philanthropist
Shibley Telhami	Israel	Scholar and Anwar Sadat Professor for Peace and Development, University of Maryland, College Park
Andrew S.W. Thomas	Australia	Astronaut
Hao Jiang Tian	China	Opera Singer
Robert Tjian	China	President of Howard Hughes Medical Institute
Ham Tran	Vietnam	Film Director
David Tran	Vietnam	CEO, Huy Fong Foods
Alex Trebek	Canada	Emmy Award-winning Game Show Host
Laurence H. Tribe	China	Constitutional Law Scholar
Satish K. Tripathi	India	President of the University at Buffalo
Chui L. Tsang	China	President of Santa Monica College
Daniel Tsui	China	Physicist and Nobel Laureate
Joseph Tusiani	Italy	Author
Victor Ukpolo	Nigeria	Chancellor of Southern University at New Orleans
Osi Umenyiora	England, UK	Football Player
Alexander Varshavsky	Russia	Biologist

Table A1 continues...

Women (n=119)		
Name	**Previous Country/Nationality**	**Profession**
Lauri Vaska	Estonia	Chemist
Srinivasa S.R. Varadhan	India	Mathematician
Abraham Verghese	India	Physician, Author, Educator
Jan Vilcek	Slovakia	Biologist and Philanthropist
Andrew Viterbi	Italy	Electrical Engineer
Eugene Volokh	Ukraine	Professor, Legal Scholar, Blogger
An Wang	China	Computer Engineer and Philanthropist
Arieh Warshel	Israel	Biochemist, Nobel Prize Winner
Elie Wiesel	Romania	Author and Nobel Laureate
Zygi Wilf	Germany	Owner of Minnesota Vikings
Simon Winchester	England, UK	Author
Richard Wolfe	England, UK	Executive Editor of MSNBC.com
James Wolfensohn	Australia	Banker
Joe Wong	China	Comedian
Martin Yan	China	Chef
Chen-Ning Yang	China	Physicist and Nobel Laureate/Professor
Jerry Yang	Taiwan	Co-Founder of Yahoo! and Philanthropist
Shing-Tung Yau	China	Mathematician
Raffi Yessayan	Lebanon	Massachusetts Superior Court Justice, Author
Fareed Zakaria	India	Foreign Policy Advisor
Paul Tiyambe Zeleza	Zimbabwe	Dean of the Bellarmine College of Liberal Arts, Loyola Marymount, CA
Elias Zerhouni	Algeria	Radiologist
Ahmed Zewail	Egypt	Chemist and Nobel Laureate

Table A1 continues…

Women (n=119)		
Name	Previous Country/Nationality	Profession
Mortimer Zuckerman	Canada	Business Leader and Philanthropist
Pinchas Zukerman	Israel	Violinist

Source: "Great Immigrants: The Pride of America" 2006-2015. Carnegie Corporation of New York. http://greatimmigrants.carnegie.org/pride-america/

Note:* Only the Egyptian nationality is used in this study (see methodology section for explanation);

** Carnegie Corporation of New York listed Iran, which might be a mistake (see methodology section for explanation).

Table A2. "Pride of America" Honorees who are Nobel Laureates, Field, Year, Race and Previous Nationality, 2006-2015

N=24			
Chemistry (n=4)		Previous	
Name	Race	Nationality	Year
Walter Kohn	White	Austria	1998
Mario Molina	White	Mexico	1995
Arieh Warshel	White	Israel	2013
Ahmed Zewail	White	Egypt	1999
Peace (n=3)			
Henry Kissinger	White	Germany	1973
Bernard Lown	White	Lithuania	1985
Elie Wiesel	White	Romania	1986
Physics (n=9)			
Willard Boyle	White	Canada	2009
Albert Einstein	White	Germany	1921
Riccardo Giacconi	White	Italy	2002
Ivar Giaever	White	Norway	1973
Charles K. Kao	Asian	China	2009
Tsung-Dao Lee	Asian	China	1957
Yoichiro Nambu	Asian	Japan	2008
Daniel Tsui	Asian	China	1998
Chen-Ning Yang	Asian	China	1957
Physiology or Medicine (n=8)			
Elizabeth Blackburn	White	Australia	2009
Günter Blobel	White	Germany	1999
Roger Guillemin	White	France	1977
Eric Kandel	White	Austria	2000

Table A2 continues…

N=24			
Chemistry (n=4)		Previous	
Name	Race	Nationality	Year
Har Gobind Khorana	Asian	India	1968
Oliver Smithies	White	England, UK	2007
Thomas C. Südhof	White	Germany	2013
Jack Szostak	White	England, UK	2009

Source: "Nobel Prizes 2015," Nobelprize.org. http://www.nobelprize.org/nobel_prizes/lists/year/index.html?year=2015&images=yes; See methodology for racial classifications.

Table A3. Net Worth of Carnegie Corporation of New York's "Pride of America" Honorees, by Sex and Race, 2006-2015
n=122

Women

White (n=27)	Net Worth		Previous Nationality
Madeleine Albright	10,000,000	http://www.celebritynetworth.com/richest-politicians/democrats/madeleine-albright-net-worth/	Czech Repub.
Anousheh Ansari	750,000,000	http://www.anoushehansari.com/about.php	Iran
Lidia Bastianich	3,750,000	http://www.celebritynetworth.com/richest-celebrities/richest-celebrity-chefs/lidia-bastianich-net-worth/	Croatia
Safra Catz	525,000,000	http://www.celebritynetworth.com/richest-businessmen/ceos/safra-catz-net-worth/	Israel
Sheena Easton	15,000,000	http://www.celebritynetworth.com/richest-celebrities/singers/sheena-easton-net-worth/	Scotland, UK
Gloria Estefan	500,000,000	http://www.celebritynetworth.com/richest-celebrities/singers/gloria-estefan-net-worth/	Cuba
Salma Hayek	85,000,000	http://www.celebritynetworth.com/richest-celebrities/actors/salma-hayek-net-worth/	Mexico
Teresa Heinz	200,000,000	http://www.celebritynetworth.com/richest-politicians/democrats/teresa-heinz-kerry-net-worth/	Mozambique
Carolina Herrera	100,000,000	http://www.celebritynetworth.com/richest-businessmen/richest-designers/carolina-herrera-net-worth/	Venezuela
Ariannna Huffington	50,000,000	http://www.celebritynetworth.com/richest-politicians/democrats/arianna-huffington-net-worth/	Greece
Marie-Josée Kravis	2,350,000,000	http://www.forbes.com/profile/henry-kravis/	Canada
Heidi Klum	70,000,000	http://www.celebritynetworth.com/richest-celebrities/models/heidi-klum-net-worth/	Germany
Mila Kunis	30,000,000	http://www.celebritynetworth.com/richest-celebrities/actors/mila-kunis-net-worth/	Ukraine
Angela Lansbury	70,000,000	http://www.celebritynetworth.com/richest-celebrities/actors/angela-lansbury-net-worth/	England, UK
Nastia Liukin	2,000,000	http://www.celebritynetworth.com/richest-athletes/olympians/nastia-liukin-net-worth/	Russia
Lara Logan	3,000,000	http://www.celebritynetworth.com/richest-celebrities/authors/lara-logan-net-worth/	South Africa
Ann-Margret	20,000,000	http://www.celebritynetworth.com/richest-celebrities/actors/ann-margret-net-worth/	Sweden
Martina Navratilova	15,000,000	http://www.celebritynetworth.com/richest-athletes/richest-tennis/martina-navratilova-net-worth/	Czech Repub.
Paulina Porizkova	10,000,000	http://www.celebritynetworth.com/richest-celebrities/models/paulina-porizkova-net-worth/	Czech Repub.
Sara Ramirez	5,000,000	http://www.celebritynetworth.com/richest-celebrities/singers/sara-ramirez-net-worth/	Mexico
Helen Reddy	3,000,000	http://www.celebritynetworth.com/richest-celebrities/singers/helen-reddy-net-worth/	Australia
Ileana Ros-Lehtinen	957,504	http://www.washingtonpost.com/wp-srv/business/congress-members-worth/	Cuba
Ariadna Thalia Sodi Miranda	50,000,000	http://www.celebritynetworth.com/richest-celebrities/singers/thalia-mottola-net-worth/	Mexico

Table A3 continues...
Women

White (n=27)	Net Worth		Previous Nationality
Charlize Theron	110,000,000	http://www.celebritynetwork.com/richest-celebrities/actors/charlize-theron-net-worth/	South Africa
Tracey Ullman	115,000,000	http://www.celebritynetwork.com/richest-celebrities/tracey-ullman-net-worth/	England, UK
Sofia Vergara	100,000,000	http://www.celebritynetwork.com/richest-celebrities/models/sofia-vergara-net-worth/	Colombia
Anna Wintour	35,000,000	http://www.celebritynetwork.com/richest-businessmen/richest-designers/anna-wintour-net-worth/	England, UK

Asian (n=6)			
Elaine Chao	11,400,000	https://www.washingtonpost.com/news/fact-checker/wp/2014/05/22/how-did-mitch-mcconnells-net-worth-soar/	Taiwan
Mazie Hirono	2,553,523	https://www.opensecrets.org/pfds/summary.php?year=2012&cid=N00028139	Japan
Bai Ling	3,000,000	http://www.celebritynetwork.com/richest-celebrities/actors/bai-ling-net-worth/	China
Loida Nicolas-Lewis	600,000,000	http://www.celebritynetwork.com/richest-businessmen/ceos/loida-nicolas-lewis-net-worth/	Philippines
Indra Nooyi	131,000,000	http://www.cnbc.com/2014/04/29/worlds-highest-net-worth-selfie-1-trillion-in-one-shot.html	India
Yoko Ono	500,000,000	http://www.celebritynetwork.com/richest-celebrities/yoko-ono-net-worth/	Japan

Black (n=2)			
Iman Mohamed Abdulmajid	30,000,000	http://www.celebritynetwork.com/richest-celebrities/models/iman-net-worth/	Somalia
Sanya Richards-Ross	1,500,000	http://www.celebritynetwork.com/richest-athletes/olympians/sanya-richardsross-net-worth/	Jamaica

Men

White (n=56)			Previous
Name	Net Worth		Nationality
Mario Andretti	100,000,000	http://www.celebritynetwork.com/richest-athletes/race-car-drivers/mario-andretti-net-worth/	Italy
Paul Anka	60,000,000	http://www.celebritynetwork.com/richest-celebrities/singers/paul-anka-net-worth/	Canada
Reza Aslan	3,000,000	http://www.celebritynetwork.com/richest-celebrities/authors/reza-aslan-net-worth/	Iran
Ralph Baer	5,000,000	http://www.celebritynetwork.com/richest-celebrities/authors/ralph-baer-net-worth/	Germany
Mikhail Baryshnikov	45,000,000	http://www.celebritynetwork.com/richest-celebrities/mikhail-baryshnikov-net-worth/	Latvia
Sergey Brin	36,300,000,000	http://www.forbes.com/profile/sergey-brin/	Russia
Martin Brodeur	55,000,000	http://www.celebritynetwork.com/richest-athletes/hockey/martin-brodeur-net-worth/	Canada
Pierce Brosnan	80,000,000	http://www.celebritynetwork.com/richest-celebrities/actors/pierce-brosnan-net-worth/	Ireland

Table A3 continues...
Men

White (n=56) Name	Net Worth		Previous Nationality
Alan Cumming	5,000,000	http://www.celebritynetworth.com/richest-celebrities/actors/alan-cumming-net-worth/	Scotland, UK
Tony Dovolani	2,000,000	http://www.celebritynetworth.com/richest-celebrities/models/tony-dovolani-net-worth/	Kosovo
Albert Einstein	1,000,000	http://www.celebritynetworth.com/richest-businessmen/richest-designers/albert-einstein-net-worth/	Germany
Craig Ferguson	30,000,000	http://www.celebritynetworth.com/richest-celebrities/craig-ferguson-net-worth/	Scotland, UK
Stanley Fischer	56,000,000	http://www.businessinsider.com/stan-fischer-net-worth-holdings-2014-2	Israel
Miloš Forman	20,000,000	http://www.celebritynetworth.com/richest-celebrities/directors/milos-forman-net-worth/	Czech Repub.
Michael J. Fox	65,000,000	http://www.celebritynetworth.com/richest-celebrities/actors/michael-j-fox-net-worth/	Canada
Peter Frampton	30,000,000	http://www.celebritynetworth.com/richest-celebrities/rock-stars/peter-frampton-net-worth/	England, UK
Frank Gehry	50,000,000	http://www.celebritynetworth.com/richest-businessmen/richest-designers/frank-gehry-net-worth/	Canada
Wayne Gretzky	200,000,000	http://www.celebritynetworth.com/richest-athletes/hockey/wayne-gretzky-net-worth/	Canada
Andrew S Grove	500,000,000	http://www.celebritynetworth.com/richest-businessmen/business-executives/andrew-grove-net-worth/	Hungary
Carlos Gutierrez	51,569,013	https://www.opensecrets.org/pfds/summary.php?cid=N99999961&year=2004	Cuba
Christopher Hitchens	2,000,000	http://www.celebritynetworth.com/richest-celebrities/authors/christopher-hitchens-net-worth/	England, UK
Khaled Hosseini	5,000,000	http://www.celebritynetworth.com/richest-celebrities/authors/khaled-hosseini-net-worth/	Afghanistan
Fred Kavli	600,000,000	http://articles.latimes.com/2013/nov/23/local/la-me-fred-kavli-20131123	Norway
Henry Kissinger	10,000,000	http://www.celebritynetworth.com/richest-politicians/henry-kissinger-net-worth/	Germany
John W. Kluge	6,500,000,000	http://www.readthehook.com/66663/john-kluge-benevolent-billionaire-goes-out-style	Germany
Ted Koppel	15,000,000	http://www.celebritynetworth.com/richest-celebrities/actors/ted-koppel-net-worth/	England, UK
Tom Lantos	4,951,512	http://www.opensecrets.org/pfds/summary.php?year=2005&cid=N00007382	Hungary
John Alberto Leguizamo	25,000,000	http://www.celebritynetworth.com/richest-celebrities/richest-comedians/john-leguizamo-net-worth/	Colombia
Ivan Lendl	40,000,000	http://www.celebritynetworth.com/richest-athletes/richest-tennis/ivan-lendl-net-worth/	Czech Repub.
Rich Little	5,000,000	http://www.celebritynetworth.com/richest-celebrities/actors/rich-little-net-worth/	Canada
Melquiades Martinez	1,200,000	http://www.floridatrend.com/print/article/5135	Cuba
Dave Matthews	300,000,000	http://www.celebritynetworth.com/richest-celebrities/rock-stars/dave-matthews-net-worth/	South Africa
Lorne Michaels	350,000,000	http://www.celebritynetworth.com/richest-businessmen/producers/lorne-michaels-net-worth/	Canada
Paul Merage	900,000,000	http://www.forbes.com/profile/merage/	Iran
Elon Musk	11,700,000,000	http://www.forbes.com/profile/elon-musk/	South Africa
Rupert Murdoch	12,600,000,000	http://www.forbes.com/profile/rupert-murdoch/	Australia

Table A3 continues…
Men

White (n=56)			Previous
Name	Net Worth		Nationality
Mike Myers	175,000,000	http://www.celebritynetworth.com/richest-celebrities/actors/mike-myers-net-worth/	Canada
Joseph Neubauer	604,000,000	http://www.forbes.com/lists/2006/12/DZ24.html	Israel
Mike Nichols	20,000,000	http://www.celebritynetworth.com/richest-celebrities/directors/mike-nichols-net-worth/	Germany
Pierre Omidyar	8,000,000,000	http://www.forbes.com/profile/pierre-omidyar/	France
Frank Oz	20,000,000	http://www.celebritynetworth.com/richest-celebrities/actors/frank-oz-net-worth/	England, UK
Jorge Ramos	12,000,000	http://www.celebritynetworth.com/richest-celebrities/authors/jorge-ramos-net-worth/	Mexico
Oscar de la Renta	200,000,000	http://www.celebritynetworth.com/richest-businessmen/richest-designers/oscar-de-la-renta-net-worth/	Dominican Republic
Morley Safer	10,000,000	http://www.celebritynetworth.com/richest-celebrities/actors/morley-safer-net-worth/	Canada
Carlos Santana	40,000,000	http://www.celebritynetworth.com/richest-celebrities/rock-stars/carlos-santana-net-worth/	Mexico
Fayez Sarofim	1,690,000,000	http://www.forbes.com/profile/fayez-sarofim/	Egypt
Arnold Schwarzenegger	300,000,000	http://www.celebritynetworth.com/richest-politicians/republicans/arnold-schwarzenegger-net-worth/	Austria
Gene Simmons	300,000,000	http://www.celebritynetworth.com/richest-celebrities/rock-stars/gene-simmons-net-worth/	Israel
Yakov Smirnoff	20,000,000	http://www.celebritynetworth.com/richest-celebrities/richest-comedians/yakov-smirnoff-net-worth/	Ukraine
Charles Simonyi	1,670,000,000	http://www.forbes.com/profile/charles-simonyi/	Hungary
George Soros	24.500,000,000	http://www.forbes.com/profile/george-soros/	Hungary
Alex Trebek	50,000,000	http://www.celebritynetworth.com/richest-celebrities/alex-trebek-net-worth/	Canada
Andrew Viterbi	420,000,000	http://ocbj.media.clients.ellingtoncms.com/static/sdbj/supplements/SDWealthiest09.pdf	Italy
Elie Wiesel	5,000,000	http://www.celebritynetworth.com/richest-celebrities/authors/elie-wiesel-net-worth/	Romania
Zygi Wilf	1,300,000,000	http://www.celebritynetworth.com/richest-businessmen/zygi-wilf-net-worth/	Germany
Mortimer Zuckerman	2,500,000,000	http://www.forbes.com/profile/mortimer-zuckerman/	Canada
Asian (n=21)			
Preet Bharara	1,700,000	http://www.vanityfair.com/news/new-establishment-2014/preet-bharara	India
Anh "Joseph" Cao	827,512	http://www.opensecrets.org/pfds/summary.php?year=2010&cid=N00030339	Vietnam
Steve Chen	350,000,000	http://www.celebritynetworth.com/richest-businessmen/ceos/steve-chen-net-worth/	Taiwan
John Cho	16,000,000	http://www.celebritynetworth.com/richest-celebrities/actors/john-cho-net-worth/	South Korea
Deepak Chopra	20,000,000	http://www.celebritynetworth.com/richest-celebrities/deepak-chopra-net-worth/	India
Rajat Gupta	130,000,000	http://dealbook.nytimes.com/2014/06/13/ex-goldman-director-guptas-last-days-of-freedom/?_r=0	India
Vinod Khosla	1,720,000,000	http://www.forbes.com/profile/vinod-khosla/	India
Daniel Dae Kim	6,000,000	http://www.celebritynetworth.com/richest-celebrities/actors/daniel-dae-kim-net-worth/	South Korea

Table A3 continues...
Men

White (n=56) Name	Net Worth		Previous Nationality
Jim Yong Kim	5,000,000	http://www.investopedia.com/articles/personal-finance/081315/jim-yong-kim-success-story-net-worth-education-top-quotes.asp	South Korea
Ang Lee	32,000,000	http://www.celebritynetworth.com/richest-celebrities/directors/ang-lee-net-worth/	Taiwan
Yo-Yo Ma	20,000,000	http://www.celebritynetworth.com/richest-celebrities/yo-yo-ma-net-worth/	France
Aasif Mandvi	800,000	http://www.celebritynetworth.com/richest-celebrities/actors/aasif-mandvi-net-worth/	India
Satya Nadella	45,000,000	http://www.celebritynetworth.com/richest-businessmen/ceos/satya-nadella-net-worth/	India
Masi Oka	5,000,000	http://www.celebritynetworth.com/richest-celebrities/actors/masi-oka-net-worth/	Japan
Vikram Pandit	60,000,000	http://www.celebritynetworth.com/richest-businessmen/ceos/vikram-pandit-net-worth/	India
I.M. Pei	20,000,000	http://www.celebritynetworth.com/richest-businessmen/richest-designers/m-pei-net-worth/	China
M. Night Shyamalan	50,000,000	http://www.celebritynetworth.com/richest-celebrities/directors/m-night-shyamalan-net-worth/	India
Patrick Soon Shiong	12,400,000,000	http://www.forbes.com/profile/patrick-soon-shiong/	South Africa
An Wang	1,600,000,000	http://articles.sun-sentinel.com/1990-03-25/news/9001310328_1_wang-laboratories-core-memory-computer	China
Jerry Yang	1,740,000,000	http://www.forbes.com/profile/jerry-yang/	Taiwan
Fareed Zakaria	4,000,000	http://www.celebritynetworth.com/richest-celebrities/actors/fareed-zakaria-net-worth/	India
Black (n=10)			
Freddy Adu	12,000,000	http://www.celebritynetworth.com/richest-athletes/richest-soccer/freddy-adu-net-worth/	Ghana
Patrick Ewing	85,000,000	http://www.celebritynetworth.com/richest-athletes/nba/patrick-ewing-net-worth/	Jamaica
Adonal Foyle	20,000,000	http://www.celebritynetworth.com/richest-athletes/nba/adonal-foyle-net-worth/	Saint Vincent and the Grenadines
Djimon Hounsou	12,000,000	http://www.celebritynetworth.com/richest-celebrities/actors/djimon-hounsou-net-worth/	Benin
Pedro Martinez	70,000,000	http://www.celebritynetworth.com/richest-athletes/richest-baseball/pedro-martinez-net-worth/	Dominican Republic
Dikembe Mutombo	75,000,000	http://www.celebritynetworth.com/richest-athletes/nba/dikembe-mutombo-net-worth/	Dem Rep of Congo
Hakeem Olajuwon	200,000,000	http://www.celebritynetworth.com/richest-athletes/nba/hakeem-olajuwon-net-worth/	Nigeria
David Ortiz	45,000,000	http://www.celebritynetworth.com/richest-athletes/richest-baseball/david-ortiz-net-worth/	Dominican Republic
Albert Pujols	90,000,000	http://www.celebritynetworth.com/richest-athletes/richest-baseball/albert-pujols-net-worth/	Dominican Republic
Osi Umenyiora	7,000,000	http://www.celebritynetworth.com/richest-athletes/nfl/osi-umenyiora-net-worth/	England, UK

Source: See methodology section and the links provided in the tables above.

INDEX

A

African Americans, 109, 119
Aggregate data, 60
American Indian, 23, 24, 26, 32, 37, 48, 52, 60, 72, 83, 86, 98
Asimov, Isaac, 10, 130
Atlantic Ocean, 14, 15

B

Bangladesh, 20, 31, 33, 40, 42, 46, 138
Black immigrants, 23, 111
Brazil, 40, 105, 114

C

China, 13, 16, 31, 32, 33, 34, 40, 41, 42, 43, 46, 47, 91, 101, 102, 111, 113, 125, 126, 127, 129, 131, 132, 133, 134, 135, 137, 139, 140, 142, 145, 148
Columbia University, 71, 72, 73, 75, 77, 79, 81, 110, 114
Coptic Christians, 106
Cornell University, 73, 77, 81, 110
Czech Republic, 33, 42, 88, 96, 97, 101, 103, 125, 128, 132, 134, 135

D

Democratic Republic of Congo, 19, 33, 41, 43, 46
Dominican Republic, 32, 33, 43, 46, 102, 103, 126, 132, 135, 137, 147, 148

E

Eastern Europe, 39, 85, 87, 88, 89, 92, 94, 96, 97, 99, 100

Einstein, Albert, 10, 13, 132, 142, 146

Eritrea, 18, 34, 41, 43, 46, 134
Ethiopia, 32, 34, 40, 41, 43, 136, 138
European Caucasian ancestry, 20

F

Federal Data on Race and Ethnicity, 20, 105, 121
Forbes Magazine, 21, 103, 115, 123
Foreign Account Tax Compliance Act, 17
Fortune 500 CEOs, 110, 123

G

GDP Purchasing Power Parity, 106, 116
General Electric, 17
George Washington University, 71, 72, 74, 77, 79
Germany, 13, 15, 16, 17, 31, 32, 34, 40, 43, 88, 89, 90, 96, 98, 101, 103, 113, 125, 126, 127, 129, 130, 131, 132, 133, 134, 136, 137, 139, 140, 142, 143, 144, 145, 146, 147

H

Haiti, 32, 34, 41, 43, 125, 133, 138
Harvard University, 72, 73, 75, 77, 79, 80, 81, 109, 110, 114
Hispanics, 109, 117
Humanities, 51, 52, 55, 118

I

IBM, 17

J

Jamaica, 32, 34, 43, 102, 127, 128, 130, 132, 145, 148

Japan, 17, 32, 34, 40, 43, 46, 89, 90, 97, 101, 102, 126, 127, 128, 136, 137, 142, 145, 148

M

Massachusetts Institute of Technology, 73, 77, 81, 109, 114, 137
McGill University, 73, 80, 81
Merage, Paul, 21, 136, 146
Microsoft, 17, 136

N

National Science Foundation, 109, 122, 123
Nativity, 106, 107, 122
New School for Social Research, 74, 81
Nigeria, 32, 35, 40, 41, 44, 102, 129, 137, 139, 148
Nobel Prizes, 10, 11, 71, 115, 120, 143
North Africa, 20
Norway, 17, 35, 41, 44, 85, 92, 103, 105, 133, 134, 142, 146

O

One-Thousand-Talent program, 16

P

Poland, 35, 44, 85, 88, 89, 90, 92, 96, 97, 128, 129, 131, 138
Pride of America, iv, v, vi, vii, 9, 13, 17, 22, 23, 24, 25, 26, 27, 28, 30, 31, 33, 36, 37, 38, 39, 40, 42, 47, 49, 51, 52, 54, 59, 60, 62, 70, 71, 74, 83, 84, 90, 98, 99, 100, 101, 102, 105, 106, 110, 113, 125, 141, 142, 144

R

Republican Party, 113

Russia, 31, 32, 35, 40, 41, 44, 86, 87, 89, 90, 94, 97, 103, 113, 127, 128, 129, 130, 131, 133, 134, 138, 139, 144, 145

S

Saint Vincent, 32, 35, 40, 44, 102, 132, 148
Singapore, 16, 17
Somalia, 32, 35, 41, 44, 102, 127, 145
South Korea, 16, 17, 32, 35, 40, 44, 46, 47, 85, 86, 92, 101, 102, 125, 131, 134, 135, 147, 148
Southeast Asia, 20
Stanford University, 72, 73, 76, 77, 79, 81, 110, 114
STEM degrees, 106, 114
Switzerland, 13, 17, 35, 41, 45, 86, 87, 94, 98, 127

T

Taiwan, 16, 17, 31, 32, 35, 40, 41, 45, 46, 101, 102, 125, 129, 131, 133, 134, 135, 140, 145, 147, 148
the Gold Rush, 111
Traore, Karim, ii
Tsui, Daniel C, 10, 13, 139, 142

U

U.S. Citizenship, 106, 122
United Kingdom, 10, 15, 16, 17, 40, 46, 85, 87, 89, 90, 92, 94, 98, 114
University of Oxford, 72, 76, 82, 109
University of the Witwatersrand, 73

W

Western Asia, 13, 20, 39, 89, 97, 99, 100

White, 20, 23, 24, 25, 26, 27, 28, 29, 30, 32, 33, 34, 35, 36, 38, 39, 49, 52, 54, 55, 56, 57, 58, 59, 60, 62, 63, 64, 65, 66, 67, 68, 69, 70, 74, 75, 76, 77, 78, 79, 80, 81, 82, 83, 84, 89, 90, 91, 92, 93, 94, 95, 96, 97, 98, 101, 102, 105, 113, 119, 125, 142,143, 144, 145, 146, 147, 148

World War II, 31, 113

Y

Yale University, 72, 76, 79, 80, 83, 110, 114